Reading the Riot Act

This lively collection presents a multi-disciplinary, multi-perspectival commentary explaining the what, where, and how, of the riots that the austerity-hit UK experienced during the long, hot summer of 2011. It looks beyond London and its Tottenham district where disturbances started, to locations such as Manchester and Birmingham. Parallels are drawn with Cairo during the period of the Arab Spring, and even with the Star Wars saga. The book locates the riots in historical context by looking at the previous UK riots of 1981 and 2001, looking at how news cycles and concepts such as that of 'moral panic' have changed in the age of social networking. It is essential reading for anyone interested in contemporary debates in social policy, media studies, anthropology, sociology, cultural studies, and human geography.

This book was originally published as a special issue of the *Journal for Cultural Research*.

Rupa Huq was Senior Lecturer in Sociology at Kingston University, UK, from 2004 until her election as Labour MP for Ealing Central and Acton in May 2015. Her previous books include *Beyond Subculture: youth, pop and identity in a postcolonial world* (Routledge, 2006) and *Making Sense of Popular Culture* (Bloomsbury, 2013).

Reading the Riot Act

Reflections on the 2011 urban disorders in England

Edited by
Rupa Huq

LONDON AND NEW YORK

First published 2016
by Routledge
2 Park Square, Milton Park, Abingdon, Oxon, OX14 4RN, UK

and by Routledge
711 Third Avenue, New York, NY 10017, USA

Routledge is an imprint of the Taylor & Francis Group, an informa business

© 2016 Taylor & Francis

All rights reserved. No part of this book may be reprinted or reproduced or utilised in any form or by any electronic, mechanical, or other means, now known or hereafter invented, including photocopying and recording, or in any information storage or retrieval system, without permission in writing from the publishers.

Trademark notice: Product or corporate names may be trademarks or registered trademarks, and are used only for identification and explanation without intent to infringe.

British Library Cataloguing in Publication Data
A catalogue record for this book is available from the British Library

ISBN 13: 978-1-138-64838-8

Typeset in Trebuchet
by RefineCatch Limited, Bungay, Suffolk

Publisher's Note
The publisher accepts responsibility for any inconsistencies that may have arisen during the conversion of this book from journal articles to book chapters, namely the possible inclusion of journal terminology.

Disclaimer
Every effort has been made to contact copyright holders for their permission to reprint material in this book. The publishers would be grateful to hear from any copyright holder who is not here acknowledged and will undertake to rectify any errors or omissions in future editions of this book.

Contents

Citation Information   vii
Notes on Contributors   ix

Introduction   1
Rupa Huq

1. Suburbia Runs Riot: The UK August 2011 Riots, Neo-Moral Panic and the End of the English Suburban Dream?   7
Rupa Huq

2. Once as History, Twice as Farce? The Spectre of the Summer of '81 in Discourses on the August 2011 Riots   26
Evan Smith

3. From Cairo to Tottenham: Big Societies, Neoliberal States, Colonial Utopias   46
Caroline Rooney

4. Critical Consumers Run Riot in Manchester   66
Sivamohan Valluvan, Nisha Kapoor and Virinder S. Kalra

5. Regional Narratives and Post-racial Fantasies in the English Riots   85
Gargi Bhattacharyya

6. Contexts for Distraction   100
Tom Henri and John Hutnyk

Index   119

Citation Information

The chapters in this book were originally published in the *Journal for Cultural Research*, volume 17, issue 2 (June 2013). When citing this material, please use the original page numbering for each article, as follows:

Editorial
Introduction
Rupa Huq
Journal for Cultural Research, volume 17, issue 2 (June 2013), pp. 99–104

Chapter 1
Suburbia Runs Riot: The UK August 2011 Riots, Neo-Moral Panic and the End of the English Suburban Dream?
Rupa Huq
Journal for Cultural Research, volume 17, issue 2 (June 2013), pp. 105–123

Chapter 2
Once as History, Twice as Farce? The Spectre of the Summer of '81 in Discourses on the August 2011 Riots
Evan Smith
Journal for Cultural Research, volume 17, issue 2 (June 2013), pp. 124–143

Chapter 3
From Cairo to Tottenham: Big Societies, Neoliberal States, Colonial Utopias
Caroline Rooney
Journal for Cultural Research, volume 17, issue 2 (June 2013), pp. 144–163

Chapter 4
Critical Consumers Run Riot in Manchester
Sivamohan Valluvan, Nisha Kapoor and Virinder S. Kalra
Journal for Cultural Research, volume 17, issue 2 (June 2013), pp. 164–182

Chapter 5
Regional Narratives and Post-racial Fantasies in the English Riots
Gargi Bhattacharyya
Journal for Cultural Research, volume 17, issue 2 (June 2013), pp. 183–197

CITATION INFORMATION

Chapter 6
Contexts for Distraction
Tom Henri and John Hutnyk
Journal for Cultural Research, volume 17, issue 2 (June 2013), pp. 198–215

For any permission-related enquiries please visit:
http://www.tandfonline.com/page/help/permissions

Notes on Contributors

Gargi Bhattacharyya is Professor of Sociology at Aston University, UK. She has written widely on issues of racism, sexuality, globalisation, and the war on terror. Her books include *Tales of Dark-Skinned Women* (UCL Press, 1998), *Race and Power* with John Gabriel and Stephen Small (Routledge, 2001), *Sexuality and Society* (Routledge, 2002), *Traffick* (Pluto, 2005), *Dangerous Brown Men* (Zed, 2008), and *Ethnicities and Values in a Changing World* (Ashgate, 2009).

Tom Henri studied Sociology, Social Policy and Social Work at the University of Southampton, UK. He then worked as a social worker and a social work educator before taking up a lectureship at Goldsmiths, University of London. His academic and research interests include the construction of youth as a problem, racisms, substance misuse, and how discourses of social class and nationality both inform and are reproduced by and through social work and social policy.

Rupa Huq was Senior Lecturer in Sociology at Kingston University, UK, from 2004 until her election as Labour MP for Ealing Central and Acton in May 2015. Her previous books include *Beyond Subculture: youth, pop and identity in a postcolonial world* (Routledge, 2006), shortlisted for the British Sociological Association's Philip Abrams Memorial Prize, and *Making Sense of Popular Culture* (Bloomsbury, 2013). Rupa works and lives in the suburbs where she has been for almost all of her life.

John Hutnyk is Professor of Cultural Studies and Academic Director of the Centre for Cultural Studies at Goldsmiths College, University of London, UK. He is the author of several books, including *The Rumour of Calcutta* (1996), *Critique of Exotica* (2000), and *Bad Marxism: capitalism and cultural studies* (2004). His latest work is the edited volume *Beyond Borders* (2012) and he is currently at work on a book to be called *Pantomime Terror*.

Virinder S. Kalra is a Senior Lecturer in the Department of Sociology, University of Manchester, UK. His research focuses on racism, ethnicity, and the related studies of diasporas and transnational communities. Virinder's most recent book is *Sacred and Secular Musics: A Postcolonial Approach* (2014).

Nisha Kapoor is Samuel DuBois Cook Postdoctoral Fellow in the Centre for Race, Ethnicity and Gender in the Social Sciences, Duke University, USA and Lecturer in the Department of Sociology, University of York, UK.

NOTES ON CONTRIBUTORS

Caroline Rooney is Professor of African and Middle Eastern Studies at the University of Kent, UK. From 2009 to 2012, she held an ESRC/AHRC Global Uncertainties fellowship with a research programme entitled Radical Distrust. She is currently a Global Uncertainties Leadership Fellow, conducting a programme which examines the roles played by utopian thinking and arts activism in the imagining of a common ground. Her books include *African Literature, Animism and Politics* (Routledge, 2000) and *Decolonising Gender: literature and a poetics of the real* (Routledge, 2007). With Ayman El Desouky, she is co-editor of *The Journal of Postcolonial Writing, Egyptian Literary Culture and Egyptian Modernity*, volume 47, number 4 (September 2011), and with Blake Brandes, she is the co-editor of *Wasafiri, Global Youth Cultures*, issue 72 (December 2012).

Evan Smith is a Vice-Chancellor's Postdoctoral Research Fellow in the School of International Studies at Flinders University, South Australia. He has written widely on anti-racism, immigration control, and the British labour movement. He is currently undertaking a project that compares the anti-colonial activism of the Communist Parties of Great Britain, Australia, and South Africa.

Sivamohan Valluvan is a Lecturer in the Department of Sociology, University of Manchester, UK. His research interests include race and ethnicity, nationalism and cosmopolitanism, and political philosophy. Sivamohan has published articles in the *Journal of Cultural Research* and *Social Identities*, and book chapters in *The State of Race* (2013) and *Whose Cosmopolitanism?* (2013).

Introduction

In the Shadow of the August 2011 Riots: One year on

> It's time we stopped hearing all this, you know, nonsense about how there are deep sociological justifications for wanton criminality and destruction of people's property.

Boris Johnson, visiting Clapham after the "riots" on 9 August 2011 (Glaze & Branagh 2011)

The saliency of the riots that began in Tottenham, north London with the shooting of Mark Duggan on a Thursday in August 2011 and spread to British cities including Birmingham and Manchester continues. Over a year after their occurrence, I set a brainstorming exercise amongst second year sociology undergraduate students at the Kingston University to come up with possible motivations behind the rioters' actions as an induction week "ice-breaker" in September 2012. The exercise certainly achieved what it set out to do. A year had elapsed but opinions were still fresh and it was difficult to contain the lively debate that ensued into its one hour timeslot. This special edition of *Journal for Cultural Research* attempts to go beyond kneejerk responses one might hear in the seminar room or street and instead gathers together considered, deliberative academic articles from different geographical locations and disciplinary perspectives to look at the riots one year now that the dust has settled on to some extent.

Situating the riots

British society seems to display a predilection for riot and affray in years ending with a 1. In 1981, disturbances in areas, such as Toxteth (Liverpool), Moss Side (Manchester) and Brixton (London) were labelled as "race riots" by the media as African-Caribbean young people were prominent in the disturbances – the significance of these events is explored in depth in this volume by Smith. In 2001, it was "Asian youth" who were seen as chiefly responsible when violence flared up in Bradford, Burnley and Oldham in the north-west of England. Writing of these earlier events, Ash Amin (2002, p. 9) stated

Figure 1. Morning star warning, August 2012.

By asserting a presence on their own terms within British public life, the Asian youths challenged those that want to keep them in their own minority spaces, and they unsettled the majority opinion that minorities should behave in a certain way in public (essentially by giving up all their folkloristic cultural practices). It is this disruption of the racialised coding of British civic and public culture that has made these riots politically significant.

Politics, conversely, was seen in the main to be somewhat lacking in 2011 when rioting erupted across the country again: this volume includes analyses of Birmingham (Bhattacharyya) and Salford/Manchester (Valluvan, Kapoor and Kalra) as well as the more obvious location of London (Huq) and more general analyses in the respective contributions of Hutnyk and Henri, Rooney and Smith. In some ways, race was downplayed as a motivating factor in the slew of quasi-official reports that emerged after the event (For example, three of the fastest to appear were Home Office Select Committee 2011; Morell 2011; Official Enquiry Report 2011). These were the most recorded riots ever and footage gathered from camera phones then broadcast widely on 24 h news TV and Youtube shows that youth from all different ethnic groups participated this time round.

At a recent riots conference in London, it was standard practice from paper givers to begin with, or at least include at some point of their orations, the quote above from the Mayor of London Boris Johnson.[1] This shunning of sociological explanations and by logical extension all academic analyses as worthteless in "the real world" is, of course, the response of a populist demagogue playing to the gallery to posit himself as an anti-intellectual. The essays in this collection offer a powerful collective rebuttal to such thinking. Far from all singing from the same hymn sheet, the six contributions here offer differing treatments of the subject matter of August 2011. Five of the papers came from the UK universities although a sixth hails from Australia — as far as possible as one can be from Blighty and still remain on the same planet, demonstrating that in today's networked new media era one can follow events in real time irrespective of physical distance from where they unfold. Indeed, what might at first sight look like "a little local difficulty", to use the phrase of Harold Macmillan, has effects that clearly reverberate much wider with global implications. Caroline Rooney draws comparisons between Cairo and Tottenham in her piece looking at the Arab Spring alongside the August 2011 riots. Certainly, as she and almost all of the contributors stress the riots that swept the Middle East the same year as London and the other UK cities erupted into flames were dismissed by many politicians as the actions of the mindless and moronic, yet in the Middle East, "good rioting" was seen by the west to have broken out as the prospect of the spread of neo-Liberal values was part of the deal.

Apocalyptic predictions made by some about how the riots would only repeat themselves have thankfully not come to fruition. On 3 August 2012, the long running, even if small circulation, UK Communist daily, the *Morning Star*, predicted a fresh bout of violence to flare up in British cities. In the event, such admonitions did not come to fruition. Instead, in Summer 2012, the Olympics came to the capital. The games had been won in part with the promise of "the world in one city" with London's multicultural character stressed in the bid. The celebratory tone struck by even the most usually right-wing reactionary titles of the UK tabloid press was rooted in the national pride engendered by a medal-winning tally that surpassed all expectations often with not quite stereotypically "true Brit" athletes key in winning the haul. The

---

1. "Collisions, Coalitions and Riotous Subjects: The riots one year on" at The Weeks Centre for Social and Policy Research, London South Bank University in conjunction with the Institute for Policy Studies in Education 28/9/12. Just a few weeks later, many of the same themes were probed at a session entitled "Riots: One year on: assessing the state of the nation" at the Institute for Ideas think tank Battle of Ideas event at the Barbican Centre, London with panellists including Sociology Professor Frank Furedi, David Lammy MP and *Guardian* columnist Zoe Williams 20/10/12 See http://www.battleofideas.org.uk/index.php/2012/session_detail/6754

phenomenally successful sprinter, Mo Farah, born in Mogadishu, was claimed in particular as "ours" even in normally reactionary quarters such as the *Daily Mail*. In the run-up to the games, an enormous amount of goodwill was generated in torch-bearing ceremonies, the length and breadth of the nation including all of the riot-hit locations of just a year earlier. This new-found Olympic spirit was a dramatic reversal of circumstances from 2011. Back then, a rhetoric of crisis was evoked by politicians and in old media, London looked like a zombie film in many of the media portrayals of riot-torn Britain but on BBC Newsnight, the historian David Starkey had the audacity to attribute the riots to the state of affairs he declared to be fact that "the whites have become black". Here, race and ethnicity were seen as dividing factors rather than a cause for rejoicing. What a difference a year makes.

Rapid reaction

This collection then collects research not only from London, chief focus of official attention as home of parliament and the national media, but it also includes important articles regarding the riots in Manchester/Salford and in Birmingham. Its ambit spreads to Cairo and English suburbia. We are not, of course, the first off the starting blocks in seeking to analyse these events. *Sociological Research Online* wins that award closely followed by *Safer Communities Journal* and *Thesis 11*.[2] Book length accounts have come out from David Lammy MP for Tottenham where the troubles began and in an edited volume of Briggs written from a criminological perspective. There was also a welter of official and quasi-official reports, both national and local. Not only has the speeding of up of technology in production timelines made all this possible, but rapid reaction followed from blogs and instantaneously via twitter and Facebook, in particular, which documented events as they occurred.

Probably, most opinionated of this clutch of essays is that of Hutnyk and Henri who take a Marxist standpoint to evoke concepts of the "ruling class", the "white supremacists" and the "super-elite" who they argue are responsible for acting on the same side as government forces, policy-makers, journalists and academics in youth suppression. The piece uses a Star Wars "mind tricks" metaphor and provocatively cites the culprit of "dysfunctional capitalism" for the plight of "petit bourgeois traders suffer[ing] alongside the lumpenised masses". Aiming conversely at a position of neutrality and objectiveness, Smith tells the story of the riots in historical context looking back at the similar circumstances of 1981, while at the same time itself reserving ultimate judgement as he persuasively makes the case that these earlier riots have since been used by all parties to distort and simplify "the political demands of the present".

---

2. See (i) Sociological Research Online, 16 (4) 24 Refereed Rapid Response Section: Recent Social Unrest In England at http://www.socresonline.org.uk/16/4/contents.html (ii) "Responding to the riots and social disorder of August 2011: a themed issue of *Safer Communities Journal*" January 2012 vol 11 no. 1 (iii) *Thesis Eleven*, April 2012 vol. 109 No. 1

How far these events will be a watershed or simply a flash-in-the-pan is probed by Bhattacharyya who turns to Birmingham and in looking at the case of Tariq Janann displays a healthy scepticism regarding the overall significance of the riots. Valluvan et al. look at Salford and Manchester where the rioters were overwhelmingly white. Their original take on these events incorporates both the views of Zizek and Bauman and uses quotations from Shakespeare's King Lear to ascertain to what extent the popular stereotype of these events can be bracketed together as simply "the shopping riots" holds. London is returned to in my own contribution but the focus taken is not the throbbing heart of the sprawling metropolis but instead, some of the more unfashionable suburbs on its edges which witnessed rioting. The argument is made that new social media challenges the old received wisdom of Cohen's (1972) folk devil and moral panic theory just as the notion of suburbia as a sterile and white zone where "nothing ever happens" is increasingly unsustainable. Cameron's coalition "ConDem" government foregrounds all of these accounts. Rooney evokes their confused flagship policy of the "big society" in her article.

By the one-year-on landmark, there had been extensive mass media popular cultural representation of the riots to compliment. Channel 4 had screened a docu-drama showing the Monday night of 8 August events unfolding in Clapham, inner South London.[3] This fact based drama containing its fair share of the "human" side of the disturbances (e.g. residents feeling under siege) was intercut with actual news reports. BBC2 showed a series of three lengthy documentaries revisiting the riots with actor reconstructions of eyewitness accounts gathered during an LSE/Guardian newspaper research project to mark the one year anniversary. After several weeks of feelgood Olympics and then Paralympics saturation coverage filling the nation's cathode ray screens and their flat twenty-first century equivalents, this felt like "feel-bad" viewing, if there can be such a thing. Inevitably, the show trended on Twitter on the evenings of its airing with many tweets emitted from viewers claiming that the spectre of rioters gloating about their actions onscreen (albeit ventriloquised by actors) made them feel sick, their stomachs turn, etc. and also generated blog commentary.[4] A tweet from @DrTomFlynn on 13 August for example exclaimed "I can already tell, 3 min in, that this is going to make me ANGRY #Riots". Of course, important questions about the sample selection, methods and data collection were absent from these programmes and no doubt can be batted away in the name of artistic or poetic licence.

This special edition attempts to take up the story and fill some of these gaps. In a range of different ways, then, these articles argue that after the cacophonous twitter storm, blog and Facebook overload that flared up in the

---

3. The show "London's Burning" was aired on 29/11/11 and starred David Morrissey. See http://www.channel4.com/info/press/programme-information/city-on-fire

4. For example, see http://infantile-disorder.blogspot.co.uk/2012/08/the-riots-in-their-own-words.html?utm_source=twitterfeed&utm_medium=twitter

heat of the moment have died down there is always a need for thoughtful insight from the academy on current events. They emanate not just from sociology where Valluvan et al. and myself are employed. Hutnyk and Henri are anthropologists. Smith is a historian who has conducted research in a law school and Rooney is an English Lit professor.

Scott Wilson has been the lynchpin of this project. His enthusiasm for it from the start and diligence in all aspects of gathering peer reviews which have greatly strengthened all the pieces in this collection as well as the editing process have made the whole experience of compiling this a smooth and pleasurable experience. My thanks go to him and we all hope you enjoy reading this special edition of Journal for Cultural Research.

References

Amin, A. (2002) *Ethnicity and the Multicultural City: Living with Diversity*, ESRC Cities Programme and the Department of Transport, Local Government and the Regions.

Briggs, D. (ed.) *The English Riots of 2011: A Summer of Discontent*, Waterside Press of Hook, Hampshire.

Cohen, S. (1972) *Folk Devils and Moral Panics*, MacGibbon & Kee, London.

Glaze, R. & Branagh, E. (2011) 'Residents Vent Anger at Boris Johnson', http://www.independent.co.uk/news/uk/crime/residents-vent-anger-at-boris-johnson-2334700.html

Home Office Select Committee. (2011) 'Policing Large Scale Disorder: Lessons from the Disturbances of August 2011', http://www.parliament.uk/documents/commons-committees/home-affairs/HC%201456-I%20Final%20Report.pdf

Lammy, D. (2012) *Out of the Ashes: Britain After the Riots*, Guardian, London.

Morell, G. (2011) '*The August Riots in England: Understanding the Involvement of Young People*', London: National Centre for Social Research, http://www.natcen.ac.uk/media/769712/the%20august%20riots%20in%20england%20web.pdf

Official Enquiry Report. (2011), http://www.5daysinaugust.co.uk/

Rupa Huq
Kingston University on behalf of all the contributors

Suburbia Runs Riot: The UK August 2011 Riots, Neo-Moral Panic and the End of the English Suburban Dream?

Rupa Huq

In August 2011, a chain of events unfolded that resulted in riots on Britain's streets. Yet, unlike previous comparable incidences in 1981 or 2001, it was not just symbols of authority located in city centres that sustained damage. London locations of the disorder not only included Tottenham where trouble began before its spread countrywide but Croydon and Ealing: both suburban locations far removed from the capital's core where high street stores — once the type of marker that made suburban living advantageous — were chief targets. Malcolm Wicks MP in Parliament even referred to Croydon on the night as resembling a "war zone". There appeared to have been a nasty upset to the usual expected state of affairs that Medhurst (1997, p. 244) has referred to as "what one might call the *newslessness* of suburbia ... a cornerstone of the vision of tranquillity that sold the suburban dream". This paper seeks to explore whether the moral panic set in motion by these distinctly post-millennial events indicates a decline of the inter-war suburban ideal that was seen by all political sides as the ultimate way of life to aspire to. It is argued that suburbia, once presumed to be a place of tradition and conservatism, is in fact changing on multiple fronts. Indeed, the 2011 riots raise a number of themes relevant to contemporary suburbia as do their apotheosis the 2012 Olympic games which took place a year on including globalisation, multiculturalism, consumerism and old and new media amongst others.

The Relevance of the Riots and Framing of the Suburb

Mid-80s indie music is not usually noted for its prophetic qualities but in August 2011, when reverberations of events that began with a fatal police shooting of a black man in Tottenham spread to Birmingham, Salford and Manchester, it seemed that life was imitating art — or at least the events of yesteryear in song. "Panic in the Streets of London" Mancunian warbler Morrissey declared back in 1986 in a song that paints a picture of urban dysfunction in a dystopian vision that engulfs a roll call of British cities in chaos. Unusually, however, unlike say the inner city riots of the 80s which occurred in Brixton and Moss Side on the inner ring of South London and South Manchester, respectively, London's suburban boroughs were not immune in 2011 as shops were looted, cars were overturned and both were set alight in London's outer boroughs, the much maligned suburbs. It was as if Liverpool indie band Half Man Half Biscuit's 1986 track "the Trumpton Riots", describing the incongruous situation when power is overthrown in a sleepy stop-animation village, was coming into fruition as looting and rioting made it to locations not usually associated with such disorder.

Although frequently derided, suburbia is nonetheless the site where the majority of the UK population resides — as many as 80% on the estimate of Barker (2009). In seeking to define it, it becomes rapidly apparent that suburbia is a contested term of great complexity. Despite being a spatial entity implying territorial boundedness, it is not easily pin-down-able. It refers to not just a geographical entity with a specific spatial location at the periphery of the city, but it also connotes a wider set of attitudes and social mores. Tottenham itself with its high BME numbers and social housing is at odds with its off-centre location. Hunt (2009) has commented "Tottenham and Ealing are equidistant from central London, but one is 'inner city' and the other 'suburban' [implying] privacy and respectability that celebrated the family unit ... home and garden, the wife and children". Just as there is no singular suburban experience, certainly no simplistic explanations should be advanced as to why the riots occurred. Nonetheless, if explaining how they came to penetrate distant far-flung suburbs in their advance, it is worth looking at how suburbia has been constructed past and present.

Like many variables that have preoccupied social scientists in the twenty-first century which it is argued are increasingly unfixed and characterised by fluidity (e.g. class, culture, race and youth), what passes for a "suburb" has historically varied in scope over time. Areas that were once the countryside have become suburbs (as lamented by John Betjemin) and in turn, what were originally thought to be suburbs have been swallowed up to become inner city locations. Both the classic Victorian suburbs of Upper Holloway, North London, where Grossmith and Grossmith's (1892) archetypal suburban busybody Mr Pooter resided or Brixton in the South, have now become "inner city" locales given the expanded core and reach of London. Furthermore, like the amalgam of social and cultural practices associated with Britishness itself, some of which are dubious in how "British" they actually are in origin (fish and chips, the Royal Family, etc.), British suburbs take many forms, shapes and sizes. These encompass garden cities, stockbroker-belt pads, corporation/council estate suburbia, 1930s ribbon development and post-war estates to name just a few. All versions were launched with much promise — be it as homes fit for heroes returning from fighting for king and country in wartime, brave new worlds of post-slum clearance in the quest to eradicate want, squalor and disease or blatantly speculative property developer's dream. Each has its own unique challenges and opportunities as do the cities that spawned them, which also have multiple socio-spatial, economic and political hierarchies. One constant that applies is that suburbs of all varieties appear to have attracted criticism from the outset. Early examples include the Campaign for the Protection of Rural England's pamphlets published by Clough William Ellis. In their essay intended for members of the American Geographical Society, Lowenthal and Prince (1964, p. 321) describe the English cityscape of the time as "mind-numbingly dreary to look at" largely on account of its suburban layout disdainfully labelled as "twentieth century urban England ... the pink bunglaloid of bypasses and arterial roads, the standardised monotony of the New World" (1964, p. 324). With no agreed definition of the word "suburb", we know then that the term is a loaded one which is in part based on geography and partially attitudinally constructed — more often than not inviting revulsion from cultural commentators.

As is the case with nation states, suburban boundaries are often administrative contrivances. What we now understand to be "Ealing", "Croydon" and "Kingston" are 1960s' creations after the amalgamation of a number of areas in their reformulated state as three large London boroughs following local government reorganisation. The London Borough of Croydon, for example, is highly mixed in character including phenomena such as the UK Home Office passport office at Lunar House with its legendary queues snaking around the block, classic inter-war suburban housing (e.g. Purley where the sitcom *Terry and June* was set), some large council estates (New Addington) and streets of ethnic commerce (London Road). This profile demonstrates that our idea of the suburb as bland, featureless zones of uniformity is deeply misguided. Croydon has long harboured big ambitions having bid several times for city status from 1956 onwards constantly to be knocked back. Its CR0 prefix (originally CRO) is the UK's largest post-code. The borough's New Addington and Kingston's New Malden districts have both acquired a somewhat macabre reputation for recent suburban goings-on. In Summer 2012, after a manhunt, the dead body of a missing 12-year-old girl was found in New Addington and the notorious "racist tram video" footage filmed on a mobile phone in late 2011 saw the subsequent prosecution of a woman from there after delivering a xenophobic rant on the Wimbledon to Croydon line. In New Malden, the corpse of a missing wealthy businesswoman was found in a lock-up garage also in summer 2012. Such events hint that all is not what it seems to be behind closed doors in the ostensibly sleepy suburbs with their pedestrian pace of life.

More commonly, however, among the attitudes that one associates with suburbs including narrow-mindedness and privacy (the twitching net curtains of suburbia allow one to see out but not others to see in) is also the idea that they are distinctly unnewsworthy. On 9 August, the day after the worst night of the August 2011 troubles, the major rolling news channels had live broadcast feeds from Ealing and Croydon. The piling in of camera crews to Ealing's once genteel Green could be seen as predictable given its proximity to Sky and the BBC White City Television Centre even if the circumstances were not. Again, like Kingston, it houses a mixed population. It has also for years been a favourite place for TV channel staffers to live in, film in and set fictional sitcoms in (*Happily Ever After, Goodnight Sweetheart*). The fact that it is a short hop on the tube to embassy-land in South Kensington in one direction or to Heathrow airport in the other has long made it a draw for London-stationed diplomats and airline cabin crew alike. Every time Ealing was mentioned in the media, it seemed obligatory to prefix it with the word "leafy". The solid Victorian villa housing and high Street at its nucleus was where the violence was concentrated but this core has, since its inception, been complimented by further waves of building including Edwardian redbrick, 1930 semis, suburban council cottage estates and post-war infill. The news channel version of events was that suburbs ordinarily equate with safety, middle England and middle age but in an unexpected jolt to the suburban dream, had now become besieged by marauding hordes of swarming youths, terrorising police and locals. The unforeseeability of these events was to such an extent that police in Ealing and Croydon had been deployed to other potential riot locations elsewhere.

Although 22 of the 33 London Boroughs experienced looting and rioting in August 2011, suburban Kingston managed to escape unscathed. The online edition of the *Kingston Guardian* reported with a palpable sense of self-satisfaction "rumours of offshoots of the kind of violence and lawlessness which hit Croydon, Colliers Wood, parts of Clapham Junction and other areas of London spreading to Kingston town centre were unfounded".[1] The tone seemed to be adopting the wartime "Keep Calm and Carry On" slogan in keeping with its "Don't Panic" undertones that has been widespread throughout the economic downturn, seen printed on different merchandise. The paper juxtaposed "real life" and the contrasting vision of the parallel world of social networks:

> Kebab shops served customers. Buses ran as normal. But in the minds of the thousands frantically keeping up to date on social network Twitter the whole town centre was a battle zone. A small police presence patrolled the town centre with protection outside the Bentall Centre, which was falsely rumoured on Twitter to be ablaze, boarded up or looted. Reports that JD Sports had been looted, Kingston station closed, the Penrhyn Road Kingston University campus or the Cambridge estate up in flames, also proved to be untrue.

The print edition *Surrey Comet* headline, again with one eye on disturbances that had taken place in comparable outer London boroughs such as Enfield, Croydon and Ealing, was "The day Kingston held its breath" (12 August 2011). The tone was one tinged with relief. The subtext was that it was now safe to exhale. The effect of social media had been entangled in the riots to such an extent that the *Guardian* issued a guide to tweeting them responsibly.[2] One of

---

1. Lindsell (2011) "Rumours of Kingston riot unfounded" in Kingston Guardian 9/8/11 at http://www.kingstonguardian.co.uk/news/9184590.Rumours_of_Kingston_riot_unfounded/?ref=rss&utm_source=twitterfeed&utm_medium=twitter
2. Hamilton, M. (2011) "UK riots: nine ways to use Twitter responsibly" 10/8/11 at http://www.guardian.co.uk/technology/blog/2011/aug/10/uk-riots-responsible-use-of-twitter

the reasons Kingston was mooted as a potential riot-spot was its fairly comprehensive shopping centre.

Consumer Culture

Suburbs have been accused by their critics for years of being consumerist hellholes with residents obsessed with material possessions and keeping up with the Jones. In JG Ballard's last ever novel, a fictional shopping mall literally becomes a temple of consumerism brainwashing the locals (2006, p. 64)

> every resident within sight of the M25, was constantly trading the contents of house and home, replacing the same cars and cameras, the same ceramic hobs and fitted bedrooms. Nothing was being swapped for nothing. Behind this frantic turnover, a gigantic boredom prevailed.

The passage detailing a mindless accumulation of goods for the sake of accumulation is almost identical to that of US professor Donaldson four decades earlier (1969, p. 74) who wrote "The suburban house is a museum in more than one sense. Not only does it serve to display the latest in technological products, such as electric toothbrushes, Exocycles and self rotating chairs, but it also shows off the most up-to-date cultural products". Accordingly, it was the carcasses of destroyed shops in the suburban locations that were among the most memorable images when copycat post-Duggan "looting" struck with the police severely stretched. The lack of overt political message led David Starkey in the infamous *Newsnight* appearance on 12 August 2011 to label this "shopping with violence". Within suburbs, there are also hierarchies of need. With the forces concentrated on the shops of central Croydon, there was less resource for defending off-centre locations. Some of the bigger names were able to insulate themselves: the Allders department store employed extra security guards when unofficial word filtered through the social networks earlier in the day that Croydon would be hit and managed to avoid trouble. As in Ealing (and Kingston), the police had been farmed out to other parts of London leaving shops undefended. Looters did not seem to distinguish between big and small businesses. The independent small traders (largely Asian shops) of London Road, already suffering the effects of straitened economic circumstances, were left to largely fend for themselves. Croydon North MP Malcolm Wicks in Parliament declared "there were virtually no police" along London Road and north of West Croydon station and that the thin blue line was "virtually invisible". Wicks asserted that by contrast, powerful corporations like Marks and Spencer's and Nestlé were "protected by police".[3]

Photos taken by my own hand in Ealing a day after the violence show the world famous Ealing film Studios, once purveyor of stiff upper lip true Brit

---

3.   http://www.publications.parliament.uk/pa/cm201011/cmhansrd/cm110811/debtext/110811-0001.htm

comedy films, now foregrounded by burnt out cars in the process of being lifted away by crane. Again, the motor vehicle is seen as an archetypal image of suburban existence — in the USA, even more than in the UK. The fact that cars had blazed in the disturbances again is an inversion of the usual suburban stereotype of the car that gets hosed down by kids at weekends in a family ritual. The road is being retarmaced where it had burned. Youtube fills in some of the gaps as archival history is there for all to see. When one of the residents who had tried to put out a rubbish bin fire was struck by a youth in what became a fatal blow, a murder enquiry ensued. False frozen in time by digital imaging on my camera are gatherings of gawpers on Ealing Green. There are also volunteers assembled to help clear up. The "broom armies" were a crucial part of the government's post-riot mythology in keeping with their "big society" rhetoric. In Ealing, these individuals were sent home as council contractors had done the job starting at 4 am after the trouble had faded. Behind a smashed shopfront, a hairdresser carries on regardless with no glass, evoking again a Blitz/"business as usual" spirit.

One can clearly draw a distinction here between the different phases of this drama. The initial events beginning in Tottenham on Saturday 6 August started as peaceful protest until the protesters felt that their grievances were not taken seriously and events were overtaken after nightfall by images of a Carpet-right store and London bus in flames. By Monday, looters in suburban areas including other smaller scale disturbances in Harrow and Bromley began their rampage two nights after the rolling news channels and social networking sites had spread the first images of youth in other parts of the capital ransacking stores and leaving with armfuls of stolen electrical goods and sportswear. The initial motivation — protests at Mark Duggan's killing by a police bullet the week before — receded from prominence as consumerism and simple outright condemnation surfaced. A much replayed quoted on the rolling news channels had the Ealing designer baby-wear boutique proprietor Liz Pilgrim describe the perpetrators of damage to her shop that had been cleared out "feral rats" (BBC 2011). In many respects, this felt like a thoroughly modern moral panic with hi-tech social media and rolling news facilitating the spread of actions to further localities than Tottenham. The discourse of moral debasement preached by right wing politicians was allied to the finger-pointing at consumerism as a culprit. Blackhurst (2005) argues that the under 25s are a "freeloading generation". He cites blogs and freesheet *Metro* having devalued the power of newspapers. Since then, London listings magazine *Time Out* and papers including the *Evening Standard* and *Ealing Gazette* have become giveaways and downloading films and music too (without payment where possible) has become normalised. This ideology of wanting something for nothing has arguably pervaded at every level of society including our legislators. In a webpost that went viral at the time generating over 4,000 comments, the right wing columnist Peter Oborne (2011) linked the greed of the looters to the expense-claiming MPs.

Sociological explanations were condemned by the Mayor of London Boris Johnson, a political figure who bridges arch-traditionalism (Oxford educated in classics) and neo-liberalism (his belief in the free market led him to propose an amnesty for illegal immigrants as part of his platform in his 2008 election bid, safe in the knowledge his office has no jurisdiction in the area). Nonetheless some of the big names of contemporary social theory were quick off the starting blocks to pen their opinions including Bauman (2011) and Žižek (2011) and even on BBC *Newsnight* the veteran socialist historian Eric Hobsbawm who died a year on at the age of 95.[4] Quotes from other theorists that predated the events seemed uncanny on idea of information overload and its umbilical link with consumerism. The long deceased Adorno (2001, p. 82) wrote:

> If mass culture has already become one great exhibition, then everyone who stumbles into it feels as lonely as a stranger on an exhibition site. This is where information leaps in: the endless exhibition is also the endless bureau of information which forces itself upon the hapless visitor and regales him with leaflets, guides and radio recommendations, sparing each individual from the disgrace of appearing as stupid as everyone else. Mass culture is a system of signals that signals itself. The millions who belong to the underclasses formerly excluded from the enjoyment of cultural goods but now ensnared provide a welcome pretext for this new orientation towards information. But this grandiose system of elucidation, transmission and rapid familiarization in the sudden shock of imposition destroys everything that the ideology of cultural products claims to promote so widely.

Leaflets, guides and radio recommendations have since been joined by a plethora of social media including Facebook, Twitter and the blogosphere. Information-wise, it is through the medium of social networks that news of the riots and post-riot situations was diffused with old media struggling to catch up, amply demonstrating that we live in a time of accelerated culture speeded up by technological innovation. When the criminal justice system kicked in, much more speedily than is the norm, the vast majority of those that came before the courts in all the riot locations was already known to the police with previous convictions, some having had prior involvement with gangs, although there is an unknown figure of those who were not caught. Information-wise, it was predominantly through the medium of social networks that riot news and rumours spread with old media (the camera crews) struggling to catch up. The post-riot match analysis demonstrates accelerated culture speeded up by technological innovation on multiple fronts. Youtube too allowed us to gawp at close range at the happenings without being there. Amongst viral hits was the "brave Hackney lady" or fallen cyclist whose rucksack was pilfered from behind — more of whom below. My photos taken the day after show the spectacle of the damage the next day which makes it look like an exhibition. Some young people take pictures of each other smiling amongst the wreckage. These become almost tantamount to alternative tourist sites, which Ealing has

---

4. See http://www.historyandpolicy.org/opinion/opinion_89.html

very few of anyway. Instead of Big Ben, it is a shattered Starbucks that people pose outside. Other pictures of the same scenes taken seconds after tell a different story: head-scratching is in evidence local traders figure out how to "make good" the damage, replacing smashed windows with boarded up facades.

Jhally (1990, p. 3) has written "To avoid … the ultimate demise of capitalism through a depressed economy, manufacturers have to ensure that what is produced is consumed. Advertising is the main weapon the manufacturers use … To this end advertising works to create false needs in people". The suburbs were themselves launched with advertising campaigns which reached their peak in the inter-war years. Ealing's still used soubriquet "the queen of the suburbs" was a marketing slogan from Victorian times constructing it as an antidote to the evils of the city. As an exhibition on the subject of suburbia that ran at the London Transport Museum in 2009 graphically displayed in old posters and marketing pitches, easy and affordable transport was always a key attraction to suburban living. Good travel connections might help to explain the chosen sites. Ealing and Croydon, as transport termini served by numerous lines. Both to some extent qualify as London subregional hubs that draw in populations from neighbouring areas. In the cacophonous jumble of voices at the post-mortem meetings, the unpreparedness of the police who were caught short-handed came over strongly, a message to the government's attempt to force through cuts to officer numbers. In Ealing at the extraordinary council meeting of 11 August, Conservative group leader Jason Stacey commented "it was like trying to fight an inferno with a water pistol". Initial post-code analyses of the first 322 suspects charged with offences showed that the average distances travelled between rioters' homes and the location of their offence was highest in suburban Croydon and Ealing — 6.9 km in the latter — but shortest in inner-London Camden and Peckham where it was between 1 and 2 km (Gainsbury 2011). In a conference held in October 2011, Local Government Minister Eric Pickles declared "Understanding how a young person — uneducated, unemployed — could come to think it's acceptable to trash their own high street, and make their neighbours' lives misery, has to be part of the response".[5] Yet, it is mistaken to assume that all of the perpetrators of rioting in any given location were living in that area as they were a highly mobile category.

The Post-Race Riots?

Escapism was an idea central to many early analyses of the suburb: it allowed those who settled there to flee the ills of the city; with its associated insalubriousness and (implicitly although not stated in marketing literature) its ethnic populations. Yet, the old ideals of the suburbs as "'bourgeois utopia' of

---

5. http://www.communities.gov.uk/speeches/localgovernment/2018326

leisure, neighbourliness, prosperity and family life" (Fishman 1989, p. 25) where domesticity reigns seems to have passed long ago, crushed under the weight of the dual-earner economy. Whilst previous twentieth-century writers have outlined the classic urban/suburban displacement motivation of "white flight" in which those with money escaped to the suburbs leaving the inner cities to minorities, one can now trace similar spatial journeys made by ethnic minorities (from inner city to suburb and within suburbia) which can be termed "brown flight", a specific form of class mobility which comes with corresponding "ethnic vote". In exercising this, suburban Asian electors helped New Labour to power in seats that the party had never taken before including outer seats London Harrow West and Brent North gained in Labour's 1997 landslide and kept by the party ever since, even if the Iraq war squandered some of the goodwill towards the party in Muslim seats. The case of Jewish suburban populations — such as from the East End to Stanmore in London or Cheetham Hill to Bury in Greater Manchester — provides earlier precedent of this diasporic suburbanisation.

Notions of a post-racial world have been widespread following the election of Barack Obama. Lentin (in press) rejects this idea arguing that it rests on a belief in the end of racism which is very much with us. Claims of August 2011 as witnessing post-race riots may at first sight seem misplaced given that the spiral of events began with a police shooting of a black man bringing up a range of related issues including disproportionate use of stop and search powers by police towards minorities, but they could be termed "post-race" for the fact that not just one ethnic group but people from minority and white majority communities were both perpetrators and victims, as they have been in most of great multicultural crises of our times such as 9-11 and 7-7. In a BBC2 programme based on the *Guardian*/LSE research interview study, it was claimed that usual gangland hostilities had been suspended for the night. On BBC's old media *Newsnight* discussion, historian Professor David Starkey openly stated Powellite 'them' vs. 'us' opinions. This argument seems hopelessly blinkered as well as needlessly inflammatory: multiculturalism is given in the suburbs as well as the inner city now and for the most part, multiple different groups coexist without regular recourse to ethnic cleansing style violence. Perhaps, the famous declaration by the late Robin Cook that chicken tikka masala is the national dish has been further realised as basmati becomes normalised alongside the meat and two veg.

Spewing out through old and new media alike in a way not experienced in 1981 or 2001 came new riot celebrities aplenty. Some of these were accidental heroes, brought to attention by phone camera footage and CCTV rather than through the glare of the media spotlight, who transpired as minority ethnic on closer examination. The cyclist caught up in the melee being relieved of the contents of his rucksack from behind while apparently being helped to safety by good Samaritans turned out to be an Indonesian overseas student. Demonstrating the post-2004 accession of new EU member states, there was the woman jumping to safety from a burning building in Croydon, who turned out to be Polish. A Facebook photo that became widely disseminated was the young black looter posing gangsta-style with a Tesco value big-sized bag of basmati rice.[6] Humour was also evident through the playful use of new media. "My brothers you are doing your Eid shopping early", said one tweet from a source with a comedy hijabed lady as her avatar, which I assumed to be a joke, although prosecutions have followed from Facebook incitement to riot when no riot took place and the case of the Robin Hood airport tweeter too is illustrative of the new clampdowns on social media as a result of officialdom thrown into panic. Others were more upfront to camera such as the grieving father in Birmingham pleading for sanity amongst local youth (see contribution of Bhattacharyya in this volume). In all these images, the original motive, justice for Mark Duggan, became more and more of a distant memory. What had started as a protest about police injustice against the black community had become something quite different.

In Notting Hill in 1958, or in Brixton, Southall and elsewhere in the 1980s, the disturbances were quickly dubbed "race riots". Ethnicity or the structural disadvantage of Asians and BNP provocation was also a factor in 2001 UK riots in the northern cities of Bradford, Burnley and Oldham. In 2011, there were examples of ethnic groups arming themselves throughout London: men coming out of communal prayers at the Whitechapel mosque chased away intruders as did the Turks of Green Lanes. Some high-profile examples of those convicted do not fit the image one might have of rioters in the public imagination. The words "millionaire's daughter" were common in the widespread coverage of grammar school-educated white Laura Johnson of Bromley (Richardson 2012). The fact that in CCTV footage showing her driving looters between stores in Woolwich on the night she appears to be smiling and laughing rather than acting under duress as she claimed weighed heavily against her. Since the 1990s, this private surveillance technology has increasingly captured moments of news history: the last moments of Jamie Bulger, Dodi Al-Fayed and Diana in a revolving door at the Ritz. At times, it has become news as in the case of a Coventry woman dumping a cat in a wheely bin in 2010.[6] Johnson's defence of mental illness was also rejected and she received a prison sentence. Thirty years earlier, some of the same factors were present: bits of London were ablaze, the economic backdrop was a time of recession. I remember being sent home early from my Ealing primary school. Trouble was brewing in the more obviously "ethnic" (Punjabi Sikh) Southall, three miles down the road, and the police advice was that it was coming next to leafy respectable Ealing. Such rumours proved unfounded on that occasion so the view that "it couldn't happen here" regarding Ealing remained undisturbed. When I was phoned up and warned that the word from Twitter was that Ealing would be next in August 2011, I assumed it was exaggerated speculation like last time and scoffed at the idea. Instead, we witnessed ethnic assertiveness. Sky News pictured several hundred Southall Sikhs bypassing the police in guarding their gurdawara on

---

6. See http://www.thesun.co.uk/sol/homepage/news/3109791/.html

hearing that trouble might be heading their way from Ealing — a complete reversal of 1981.

Racially inflected elements in responses to the riots were multiple. The most visible MP following the disturbances was Tottenham Labour representative David Lammy, himself black, who was thanked for his intervention in the House of Commons by David Cameron and later published a book on the subject (2011). Following the initial outbreak of violence, television pictures switched to portrayals of groups of white Caucasian males in the London suburbs of Eltham and Enfield, who had mounted vigilante protectionist fronts to defend local property. Some of these had far right links. *The Voice* reported that the vigilante patrols in Eltham were the result of "a community gathering ... hijacked by racist thugs".[7] Local MP Clive Efford was quoted as stating: "Unfortunately, members of the EDL [English Defence League] came to Eltham to cause trouble and exploit this situation against the backdrop of all the other things that are happening". In his argument that whites have become "culturally" black after multiculturalism, the Starkey line to indirectly echo the 1968 prediction of Britain's most famous racist politician Enoch Powell that racial mixing would cause necessary dischord (known commonly as the "rivers of blood" speech even if that phrase was never actually used) oversimplifies matters. As also argued in this volume by Kalra et al. in Salford, the personnel involved were mainly white. Elsewhere, the dynamic shifted throughout the evening. In Croydon, anecdotal evidence was that earlier in the evening, there had been ethnically mixed groups of youth caught up in the moment, whereas later in the evening, long established (largely white) criminal gangs of South-East London predominated, stealing to order and reportedly loading up vanfulls of white goods. The Reeves Corner furniture store that had withstood the Blitz was a celebrated casualty that had a great shock factor but their loss was to some extent mitigated by its iconic position and the proprietors' later celebrity status — for example, the Reeves family received VIP Olympics tickets having got replacement premises up and running swiftly. Many more Asian businesses of London Road comparatively suffered in silence, and to date have not received compensation.

Modern Moral Panic and the Decline of Suburbia

David Cameron having been summoned from his Tuscan sunlounger (as had his Eton contemporary Boris Johnson) remarked that these events demonstrated that society had become "sick" with moral decay. Indeed, this recourse to moral bankruptcy bolstered by a fulsome instantaneous reaction in the shape of rolling news with constant tickertape captions on News24 and SkyNews bolstered by social media and the blogosphere made this an oddly compelling

---

7. See "Far right thugs warn: 'A n****r is going to get it'," in The Voice 10/8/11 at http://www.voice-online.co.uk/article/far-right-thugs-warn-%E2%80%98-nr-going-get-it%E2%80%99

thoroughly modern moral panic, a twenty-first century version of the way 1960s seaside mods vs. rockers bust-ups multiplied via media coverage on multiple platforms.[7] A staple of sociology syllabus students for subject from GCSE onwards is the well-known theory of moral panic which has now become part of our everyday lexicon and has the subject of secondary source material many times since its first appearance. Cohen's much quoted definition in *Folk Devils and Moral Panics* (1972, p. 9) spells this out to be "a condition, episode, person or group of persons [who] become defined as a threat to societal values and interests; its nature is presented in a stylized and stereotypical fashion by the mass media; the moral barricades are manned by editors, bishops, politicians and other right-thinking people; socially accredited experts pronounce their diagnoses and solutions; ways of coping are evolved or (more often) resorted to; the condition then disappears, submerges or deteriorates and becomes more visible". Yet, such understandings of top down media functioning are in danger of looking dangerously outmoded now that the media is far more diffuse than ever before, offering opportunities for those depicted to respond to portrayals of them via citizen journalism.

As a veteran of demonstrations and protest marches of the 1990s, I initially was not sure what to make of this wave of public disorder which took place only a mile away with my home address, although whilst events unfolded, I was cowering indoors flipping between 24-h channels on TV with a laptop at my side monitoring Twitterfeeds mentioning Ealing on simultaneously. In some respects, there were similarities to the protesting movements I had been involved in during my twenties. These were mobilisations that were largely youth-led inviting comparisons with an unruly mob. The police were seen as the enemy, or at least if not a singular enemy part of the problem. Yet, as the initially anonymous walking stick-wielding "brave Hackney lady" who rose to prominence via youtube pointed out these were not people "fighting for a cause", they were instead "doing over Footlocker". The one academic theory that I cited in my earlier work on the mid 1990s opposition to the then Criminal Justice Bill and Public Order Act (Huq 1998) that seemed appropriate to the 2011 riots is Mikhail Bahktin on the carnivalesque. In common with this, the riots had elements of spectacle not just at their moment of occurrence but through their digital after effect through social media. Many of our memories of this febrile period date from the images that were captured by both the official media and citizen journalism alike. With these being the most recorded riots ever, these were both still imagery and moving footage of what was a fast-moving situation beamed around the globe in seconds. When the initial Tottenham protests of the Saturday night became more aggressive, there were reports that BBC cameras had fled the area. As the Corporation itself reported "A BBC TV news crew and satellite truck also came under attack from youths throwing missiles".[8] The image conveyed was one of lawlessness writ large and a rampaging anarchic mob. In the accompanying video, the reporter

---

8. http://www.bbc.co.uk/news/uk-england-london-14434318

filing his commentary down the phone from behind police lines describes a "dangerous and volatile ... situation", reassuring viewers that even though their satellite had its windows smashed, its operator is safe and well from the hail of bottles, bricks and petrol bombs pervading.

The term flashmob — "a large group of people who gather in some predetermined location, perform some brief action, and then quickly disperse" — seems apposite here (McFedries 2003). In some senses, the riots were unforeseeable. In the same BBC report on the initial Tottenham night of violence referred to above Borough Commander Stephen Watson is quoted as stating: "We had no information to suggest that we would have the scale of disorder that now confronts us". On the night, the micro-blogging site Twitter with its instantaneous reactions captured some of the shifting opinion in real time from warnings of where was going to "kick off" next to the day after when both Ealing and Croydon were in tweets that read "[name of riot-hit locality] is trending for all the wrong reasons," referring to the way in which trends are discerned and the word has become a verb derived from subjects that are being currently tweeted about. As the columnist Hari Kunzru observed: 'Early in the evening, watching social media, I was seeing variants of the same joke:

> I'm in Chiswick/Hampstead/Dulwich Waitrose and there's a RIOT! They've run out of POLENTA!".[9] The smug sense of disconnection (this is nothing to do with me, or my comfortable middle-class life — it is an affair of the poor, in places I choose not to go) was soon replaced by panic: 'WHERE IS THE ARMY?'

But then, in keeping with flashmob characteristics, it seemed that the "riots" in the main disappeared as quickly as they had appeared even if the hand-wringing analyses continued much further on. The more lasting effects were manifested in the swiftness of the summary justice and show-trials that ensued. At the time of the parliamentary expenses scandal, it often seemed that press commentary oscillated between outrage that MPs' claims had been either too extravagant (such as the duck-house one Tory installed on his country estate) or too petty (Home Secretary Jacqui Smith claimed for a bathplug and Hazel Blears a Kit Kat bar). After the riot sentencing began, the usual commentariat aftermath ensued pondering whether these sentences were too excessive. A six-month custodial sentence, for example, was seen as disproportionately punitive for a first-time offence stealing bottled water[9] as was the harshness of conviction for incitement to riot on Facebook when the riot did not in the end occur. "Moral panic" seems an appropriate term as it arose from criminology and some of its early applications were around youth crime, e.g. "mugging" (Hall, Critcher, Jefferson, Clarke, & Roberts 1978) even if the nature of this and the diversity of the "folk devils" (black, white, young, old, male and female) had changed.

Politicians were quick to pronounce on the riots — even before the recall of Parliament on 11 August. The right positioned themselves in a bid to be the

---

9. http://www.guardian.co.uk/commentisfree/poll/2011/aug/12/riots-water-theft-punishment, http://www.guardian.co.uk/uk/2011/dec/07/twitter-riots-how-news-spread

most macho. The utterances of Prime Minister-by-default Cameron and the soon-to-be re-elected Mayor of London Boris Johnson rejected any explorations of wider reasons behind the actions of the rioters instead dismissing them as irrational. This approach had been tried by Conservatives earlier in time. In response to New Labour's eye-catching and ultimately vote-winning slogan "tough on crime, tough on the causes of crime" in 1993, the then Prime Minister John Major had declared "Society needs to condemn a little more and understand a little less" (MacIntyre 1993). Eighteen years later, little seemed to have changed in the blue corner. Toynbee and Walker (2012, p. 73) in their mid-term assessment of the coalition government accord the riots only a passing mention declaring "smoke billowing into a night sky during the riots of August 2011 ... choked ministers ... Cameron's Tory instincts said punish; his critics said training and employment: because austerity ruled out both extra prisons and extra support, Cameron was tongue-tied". The false economy of police cuts was also highlighted by the crisis. Extreme left blogs advanced structuralist explanations[10]. In hindsight, some said that the riots had been entirely predictable with a ring of "told you so" in their tones. The Sociological Imagination blog commented that these events had "the look of being predetermined and waiting to happen. Somebody had to throw the match for the leaking fuel tank to catch fire and explode... [the] UK disturbances are expressions of individual and collective bitterness and hatred towards a non-responsive and indifferent government that does not hesitate in using violence against them to keep a semblance of order, (Kona 2011)". Meanwhile, demonstrating his academic background Labour leader Ed Miliband offered a measured response to the riots which, unlike Cameron's apoplexy, cautioned that there was no single cause of the riots. In keeping with this logic, there was no single riot: the peaceful afternoon protest on the Saturday following Mark Duggan's death on Thursday bore little resemblance to the wholesale clearing out of designer gear from the racks of Oasis singer Liam Gallagher's "Pretty Green" flagship store in Manchester city centre on the Tuesday. Parallels were drawn with the Arab Spring, yet these looked different from other political demonstrations. There were no banners being waved or placards or sloganeering. The buildings attacked were not symbols of authority. Instead, they seemed to have been picked for the goods on their shelves, in an exercise that focused largely on the acquisition of material goods.

Adorno and his Frankfurt school colleagues stated the classic position of a fear of mass culture spreading lowbrow trash which has been repeated in various ways by others since in a what is now known as the dumbing down debate. In the same way as the age-old sociological dichotomy structure vs. agency that has been revised with Giddens (1984) concept of "structuration" which steers a course between these two extremes, the media is less monolithic than

---

10. Eg see http://socialismandorbarbarism.blogspot.co.uk/2011/08/open-letter-to-those-who-condemn_10.html, http://www.davidosler.com/2011/08/london-riots-initial-reaction/, http://www.socialistworker.co.uk/topic.php?id=102, http://thecommune.co.uk/2011/08/10/nothing-to-lose-nothing-to-win/

ever before with the boundaries between "them" (producer) and "us" (consumer) continually dissolving. It is now given that Internet access has near-universal penetration. Fears such as those voiced by van Zoonen (2001) at the beginning of the millennium warning that "the internet" had the potential to be divisive as an elitist phenomenon that could subordinate women seem now quaintly outdated having certainly not anticipated the rise, e.g. of mumsnet. Citizen journalism means that everyone can have a blog or have their voice heard in a forum. Her argument urging "a redefinition of the Internet from the exclusively masculine domain borne of the American military-industrial academic complex towards its feminine antithesis of peaceful cooperation and experimentation" has in part been realised. The Internet has the potential for humour as well as the spread of factual information. "Memes", the mickey-taking (sometimes photo-shopped, sometimes not) images that have the capacity to "go viral" rapidly, are often more memorable than the original version of events that they seek to lampoon. Halloran's famous formulation, "we should ask not what the media does to people, but what people do to the media," Halloran (1970, p. 15), is instructive here. In their riot coverage, the old media fed off new media and social networks which allowed a right of reply to the reader. Osgood and Schramm's model of communication showing an active audience and that the message is changed by the decoder is more apt here or Hall's (1973) Encoding–Decoding Theory which constructed the three categories of the dominant, oppositional and negotiated rather than binary models. Waters (2001, p. 185) has claimed that "Modern society is ... specifically reflexive in character. Social activity is constantly informed by flows of information and analysis which subject it to continuous revision and thereby constitute and reproduce it". Cyberspace in the event has turned out to be far more than the sinister accompanying apparatus of some western cultural project committed to the hegemonic spread of capitalist values.

Suburban Aftermath: Riots in Retrospect

Should we really be surprised that the issues of police incompetence that led to a death in north London (Tottenham) that spread out to the south (Croydon) and westwards (Ealing) continued like a rash beyond London's compass points to Birmingham, Manchester and beyond? Perhaps, in reality, these three locations are all examples of ethnically mixed twenty-first-century suburbs. In all three sites, a year on from the riots the Olympic Torch was paraded around the same streets that had blazed in August 2011 — a different type of flame towards which a great outpouring of goodwill followed in part obscuring some of the initial scepticism that had greeted the games (Hilary 2012). Before that were the post-riot public meetings with their soul-searching. When the criminal justice system kicked in, the vast majority of those that came before the courts in all the riot locations were already known to the police with previous convictions, some having had prior involvement with gangs, although there is an unknown figure of those who were not caught. Both national and local newspapers engaged in "one year on" retrospectives of the events in 2012.

Ealing Councillors were summoned for an emergency post-riot gathering open to the public in August in a mirror of Cameron's recall of parliament. This extraordinary session of full council was followed in October by a public meeting that would feed into the government-appointed taskforce Riots Communities and Victims Panel. Both seemed almost a cathartic outpouring as residents queued up to make short statements into the microphone to propose that the police should be given more powers or the bankers should be strung up — amongst others. At times, the discussion veered into kneejerk reactions from audience members who had not directly experienced the events but felt the need to be heard. A number of explanations were advanced including consumer capitalism, greed, unemployment and cuts to council coffers and public services — the majority of which have not fully bitten yet. In short, these aligned less with Boris Johnson's negation of sociological evidence or the Cameron line that "this was criminality pure and simple" and instead, pointed the finger at structural inequality and wider societal mores/expectations rather than individuals behaving in a manner that was "sick" (again a Cameron-ism). The bankers were singled out for criticism. The harsh sentences were also attacked from the floor by some but supported by others. The personal testimony from eyewitnesses was most moving, members of the business community and local residents who had been at home in adjoining roads described the terror they had experienced. Ealing Borough Commander Andy Rowell said that 276 arrests had been made at that point in time with more to come. Possibly because it was an invited audience of community leaders bolstered by the general public who were asked along, religion seemed to be uppermost in the analyses of the "why?" question. The leader of the Ealing bahais told us we had lost our spiritual way, for example. In Croydon, according to anecdotal evidence from a friend who attended the equivalent meeting, previous history from long ago was harked back to with slavery being blamed.

In 1987, on her third election, victory Thatcher declared that something must be done about "those inner cities", showing her disdain for the traditionally Labour-voting parts of the country. The thrust of New Labour regeneration 10 years later was focused mostly on show-piece projects in city centres — pedestrianisation here, a cutting-edge designed spaceship-like arts centre there. In turn, a revival of the reputation of the inner city — beyond the city centre's core — took place. These two rings of the doughnut began to be associated with culture, cosmopolitanism and energy — contributing to the idea of suburbia on the outer ring as being less desirable for possessing all the opposite characteristics. As a result, we have seen almost a disavowal of suburbia, which to paraphrase Goldsworthy (2005) is a location that "dare not speak its name". The current marketing from boroughs like Croydon or Labour-run Ealing repeatedly stresses their "vibrancy" in a quest to be attractive. Croydon's 2012 city bid claimed, for example, that it was "London's most vibrant borough ... where multiculturalism thrives". In the same way as suburbs have long been seen as "out of the way" places, "where nothing ever happens" and "dormitory towns", there has been a relative paucity of suburban sociology in comparison to say urban studies. If we think of stereotypical divides of suburb vs. city as stable/safe vs. risky and ethnically indigenous white vs. multicultural, the contemporary suburb increasingly resembles the old inner city while gentrification makes the inner city (much of which was once originally suburbia) more and more suburban in terms of the profile of its occupants who are frequently white professionals — Tony Blair lived in Islington before he got the keys to Downing Street and David Cameron in North Kensington. Potential danger now lurks at every turn in the contemporary suburb. The economic downturn has exacerbated matters with further public services cuts round the corner. Those in the suburbs can no longer afford to be smug but instead are fretful. Gareth Thomas MP in a pamphlet urging Labour to take suburbia seriously in its policy review terms the prevailing mood as "the politics of anxiety". It would be easy to argue that rioting and looting have sealed the status of the suburb as the new inner city but it was not riots that killed the suburban dream, fractures in its idealised prescription for life were long underway before August 2011 if ever the happy families with 2.4 children and dog scenario ever existed in the first place.

As early ago as 1994, under another deeply unpopular Conservative government accused of kneejerk responses in their policy formulation, long before the expansion of social networking McRobbie (1994, p. 23) remarked "Far from being overwhelmed by media saturation, there is evidence to suggest that these social groups and minorities [neo folk devils] are putting it to work for them", alleging eroded boundaries between the media's assumed position "on high" and those that it sought to represent with her article "Folk Devils Fight Back" initially published in *New Left Review* then available as a chapter in her 1994 book. The piece got a grudging acknowledgement in Cohen's new introduction to his third edition (2002) but not much else. Much of the information flow of what is simply in circulation, be it news or commentary on the current events, is eased now that it is free, i.e. unpaid for. Although some would say that this itself signals liberty, others are more sceptical. Blackhurst (2005, p. 58) has written: "Online we snack on small mouthfuls of information ... Constant grazing makes us lose our respect for mere words. The freewheeling online experience — opening three browsers at once and never finishing an article — punctures the authority of newspapers. Even visually, online newspapers feel less important". His claim sounds like the jealous last gasp of the old media who in a desperate bid to remain relevant all now have adopted blogs and Twitterfeeds — the latter, i.e. famous people's tweets are often a source of their "news". The way Twitter has assumed the mantle of instantaneous commentary on social issues in real time was displayed in August 2011 when graphs were published on the web illustrating the peaking of usage on the day that the riots spread most, 8 August. People like myself who were just looking in that day without even having an account would not be accounted for in such statistics. At the time of writing, it has been claimed that the 2012 Olympics saw the high point for tweets sent — a far more "good news" story than looting and burning that also commanded blanket news coverage and offstage commentary during the duration of its unfolding. Since its inception in the 1970s, the theory of "moral panic" that itself sprang from the 1960s mods vs. rockers seafront clashes serves as an example of an academic media studies/sociological term that has now passed into almost everyday language (at least in the broadsheet press in any case). Yet, both this notion and traditional understandings of what constitutes a suburb feel rather like relics of a bygone age in modern multi-ethnic double-dip Britain.

References

Adorno, T. (2001) *The Culture Industry: Selected Essays on Mass Culture*, trans J. M. Bernstein, Routledge, London.
Ballard, J. G. (2006) *Kingdom Come*, Fourth Estate, London.
Barker, P. (2009) *The Freedoms of Suburbia*, Frances Lincoln, London.
Bauman, Z. (2011) 'Fuels, Sparks and Fires: On Taking to the Streets', *Thesis Eleven*, vol. 109, pp. 11-16.
BBC. (2011) 'London Riots: "Feral Rats" Looted My Business', http://www.bbc.co.uk/news/uk-england-london-14456964 (accessed 9 August 2011).
Blackhurst, R. (2005) 'The Freeloading Generation', *British Journalism Review*, vol. 16, pp. 53-59.
Cohen, S. (1972) *Folk Devils and Moral Panics*, MacGibbon & Kee, London.
Cohen, S. (2002) *Folk Devils and Moral Panics*, 4th edn, Routledge, London.
Donaldson, S. (1969) *The Suburban Myth*, Columbia University Press, New York, NY.
Fishman, R. (1989) *Bourgeois Utopias: The Rise and Fall of Suburbia*, Basic Books, New York, NY.
Gainsbury, S., Beranard, S. & Cukzac, N. (2011) 'Where the Riot Suspects Live', *Financial Times*, http://www.ft.com/cms/s/0/513cf864-d57b-11e0-9133-00144feab49a.html#axzz29XkTgOnw.
Giddens, A. (1984) *The Constitution of Society: Outline of the Theory of Structuration*, Polity Press, Cambridge.
Goldsworthy, V. (2005) 'The Love that Dares not Speak its Name: Englishness and Suburbia', in Rogers, D. & MacLeod, J. (eds), *Revisions of Englishness*, Manchester University Press, Manchester, pp. 95-106.
Grossmith, G. & Grossmith, W. (1892) *Diary of a Nobody*, Penguin, London.
Hall, S. (1973) 'Encoding and Decoding in the Television Discourse', *CCCS Stencilled Paper no. 7*. Birmingham: Centre for Contemporary Cultural Studies.
Hall, S., Critcher, C., Jefferson, T., Clarke, J. & Roberts, B. (1978) *Policing the Crisis: Mugging, the State, Law and Order*, Macmillan, London.
Halloran (1970:15) *The Effects of Television*, Panther, London.
Hunt, T. (2009) 'The Suburbs are Derided by Snobs, Yet They Offer Hope for Our Future', *The Observer*, http://www.guardian.co.uk/commentisfree/2009/jul/19/suburbs-snobbery (accessed 26 July 2009).
Jhally, S. (1990) *The Codes of Advertising: Fetishism and the Political Economy of Meaning in the Consumer Society*, Routledge, London.
Kona, P. (2011) 'UK Riots 2011 — A "social revolution" yet to take place?', *Sociological Imagination*, http://sociologicalimagination.org/archives/6205 (accessed 15 August 2011).

Lentin, A. (in press) 'Post-race, post politics: the paradoxical rise of culture after multiculturalism', *Ethnic and Racial Studies*.

Lowenthal, D. & Prince, H. (1964) 'The English Landscape', *The Geographical Review*, vol. 54, no. 3, pp. 309-346.

MacIntyre, D. (1993) 'Major on crime: "Condemn more, understand less",' http://www.independent.co.uk/news/major-on-crime-condemn-more-understand-less-1474470.html

McFedries, P. (2003) 'Mobs R Us' in Spectrum, *IEEE*, vol. 40, no. 10, p. 56.

McRobbie, A. (1994) *Postmodernism and Popular Culture*, Routledge, London.

Medhurst, A. (1997) 'Negotiating the Gnome Zone: Versions of Suburbia in British Popular Culture', in Silverstone R. (ed.), *Visions of Suburbia*, Routledge, London, pp. 240–268.

Oborne, P. (2011) 'The Moral Decay of Our Society is as Bad at the Top as the Bottom', *Daily Telegraph*, http://blogs.telegraph.co.uk/news/peteroborne/100100708/the-moral-decay-of-our-society-is-as-bad-at-the-top-as-the-bottom/ (accessed 11 August 2011).

Pickles, E. (2011) 'Helping the High Street recover after the riots', speech 27/10/11 delivered at LGA Riots Summit, London.

Richardson, K. (2012) 'Viewpoint: Why Laura Johnson's Riot Case Makes Parents Uneasy', http://www.bbc.co.uk/news/magazine-18193227 (accessed 26 May 2012).

Toynbee, P. & Walker, D. (2012) *Dogma and Disarray: Cameron at Half Time*, Granta Books, London.

Van Zoonen, L. (2001) 'Feminist Internet Studies', *Feminist Media Studies,* vol. 1, no. 1, pp. 67-72.

Waters, M. (2001) *Globalisation*, 2nd edn, Routledge, London.

Žižek, S. (2011) 'Shoplifters of the World Unite', *London Review of Books*, http://www.lrb.co.uk/2011/08/19/slavoj-zizek/shoplifters-of-the-world-unite (accessed 19 August 2011).

Once as History, Twice as Farce? The Spectre of the Summer of '81 in Discourses on the August 2011 Riots

Evan Smith

The riots which occurred in August 2011 across Britain happened thirty years after the riots that swept the country in the spring and summer of 1981. In the discourses that emerged surrounding the 2011 events, many commentators made comparison between the contemporary disturbances and those that occurred in 1981. This article examines two arguments that emerged out of the comparison between the two events. Firstly, a consensus seemed to have been reached concerning the causes, motives and actions of the 1981 riots, particularly, that the 1981 events were a "legitimate" form of protest against police harassment and institutional racism. This was supposedly in contrast to the "criminality" of those involved in the 2011 events, with the suggestion that those who were rioting nowadays had no legitimate grievances to rebel against. Secondly, amongst those had sympathies with those in "rebellion"; a consensus was formed that the events of August 2011 were repetitions of those which occurred in 1981. For many on the left and within activist circles, the same neoliberal/monetarist agenda by the Tories (creating high unemployment and cuts to public services), combined with continuing institutional racism, were the underlying causes for the 2011 riots and those of the 1980s, and the lessons of the battles against Thatcherism were to be heeded. This article will show how the history of the riots of the 1980s were used by various commentators on the left and the right to interpret why the events of August 2011 happened and what the response to these events should have been. The article will propose that while historical comparisons are useful, the problem of these discourses of the 2011 riots was that they were primarily seen through a historical prism that depended on an interpretation of the history of Britain in the 1980s under Margaret Thatcher and this was often distorted analysis of contemporary events.

Karl Marx famously paraphrased Hegel in *The Eighteenth Brumaire of Louis Bonaparte*, saying that "all facts and personages of great importance in world history, as it were, twice", adding, "the first time as tragedy, the second as farce" (Marx 1969, p. 15). Marx's point was that in periods of great societal upheaval, many of those who observe and attempt to explain these events look to past historical events for an interpretative framework, or as Marx (1969, p. 15) put it, "they anxiously conjure up the spirits of the past to their service and borrow from them". While Marx was writing about the French counter-revolution that occurred after the uprising of 1848, these words could be used to describe any number of rebellions, revolutions or episodes of disorder. The focus of this article is on the riots that spread across the UK in early August 2011 and how most commentaries and analyses of these riots sought to explain them through the prism of the riots that occurred in the UK in 1981 (first in April in Brixton and across the UK in the summer of the same year). While Marx (1969, p. 15) wrote about how those observing the events of 1848-1851 looked back to the "Thermidor" period of the French Revolution, substituting "Caussidière for Danton, Louis Blanc for Robespierre, the *Montagne* of 1848-1851 for the *Montagne* of 1793-1795", those writing on the riots of 2011 looked back to 1981, substituting David Cameron for Margaret Thatcher, Theresa May for Willie Whitelaw and the black, white and Asian youth of 1981 for the black, white and Asian youth of 2011.

The parallels between the events of 2011 and 1981, and their surrounding socio-economic and political conditions, seem, at first glance, to be very similar. David Cameron's Conservative Government was pushing "austerity" measures to cut public spending and reduce the "debt" inherited from Labour, akin to the monetarist policies sought by the first Thatcher Government, which meant less money for the poorer sections of British society reliant on some form of government assistance and less spending on other public services in poverty-afflicted areas of the UK. In 2011, as well as thirty years ago, these austerity measures, combined with a wider globalised financial crisis, had led to great increases in unemployment, particularly amongst the UK's ethnic minority communities and amongst young people. Alongside these economic factors, both years saw concerns arise about the powers of the police, particularly in the operation of stop and searches (or "sus" laws in 1981) and the perceived targeting of ethnic minorities by the police, as well as other sections of the lower classes and young people in general.

These parallels were picked up upon by many commentators. For example, Gilroy (2011) remarked in a speech on the riots that there was "a temptation ... to say it's the same game as it was thirty years ago" and citing Stafford Scott, said that "unemployment numbers, school exclusion numbers, *stop and search numbers* [his emphasis] ... In terms of these things, the number are as bad as or worse than they were thirty years ago". In their research as part of *The Guardian* and LSE's *Reading the Riots* project, Newburn, Lewis and Metcalf (2011) wrote that the conditions for the riots of 1981 were "in many ways similar to those that blighted England this summer", pointing out that "[b]oth took place while a Conservative prime minister grappled with the effects of global economic downturn and rising unemployment". Wheatle, the novelist and participant in the 1981 Brixton riots, also wrote in The Guardian (2011) that the circumstances between the two periods of rioting were "remarkably identical", identifying factors such as "economic crisis, disenfranchised young people, deep cuts in public services and a deterioration between young black people and the police".

Even before the August 2011 riots, commentators had remarked that the socio-economic and political environment in the UK seemed to mirror that of the early 1980s, and in discussing the thirtieth anniversary of the riots of 1981, there were speculations of the possibility of riots in the near future. An article in *The Guardian* on the upcoming anniversary of the Brixton riots stated that "some community leaders are warning that similar tensions could, again, spill over into violence", describing "a toxic cocktail of factors reminiscent of 1981, including rising youth unemployment, cuts to local services and deep suspicion of the police", as well as "the politicisation of a new generation of anti-cuts protests ... and anti-tuition-fees marches" (Walker 2011). The article also quoted Alex Wheatle as saying:

> You're going into dangerous territory, eroding services for young people ... I can imagine a repeat of 1981. I can feel the anger. I can feel the resentment towards authority. You're getting a lot of young people with degrees and big debts, but not jobs. What was really striking in 1981 was the lack of hope. When you have no hope you're going to confront the police, you've got nothing to lose. (cited in, Walker 2011)

Another article on the riots in Liverpool in 1981 in *The Guardian* quoted a community worker who had experienced the riots as a youngster, who saw parallels between Liverpool in the present day and the city in the 1980s:

> First, there was deindustrialisation, now there's a recession, and you hear people worried about losing their jobs and how they will now in all probability have to work longer for their pensions. It makes some of us quite jealous, because at least you had jobs consistently enough to enable you to build a pension in the first place. I look at these people now and think to myself: "Welcome to our world. Welcome back to 1981." (cited in, Vulliamy 2011)

However, as Hughes (2011) has said, "[h]istory doesn't repeat itself exactly" and there is logic in the government assertion that 2011 is not 1981 (McSmith 2011). Many commentators and scholars have noted that there are a number of differences, both in the context from which the riots developed and how the riots actually unfolded, between the riots that have recently occurred and those that happened thirty years before. This article accepts the argument that while these riots occurred quite spontaneously, they did not arise from nowhere and were not completely unexpected, and while one cannot draw a direct line between the riots of 1981 and the riots of 2011, the history of riots, public unrest and civil disorder in the UK does show that there is a precedent for what occurred last year and the riots were not an a-historical episode. The point of this article is that while the recent history of riots that have occurred in the UK since the mid-1970s can provide us with an insight into the most recent outbreak of urban unrest, much of the discourse on the 2011 riots was presented through the prism of 1981. On one hand, the events of 1981 were upheld by some commentators (mostly on the centre-right, but some on the centre-left) to contrast the "criminality" of those participating the most recent riots with the more "political" and "socially aware" riots of the early 1980s. On the other hand, there seemed to be a number of people, particularly on the left, who saw a teleological narrative that formed a direct connection between the events of 1981 with the present era, putting forward that the lessons of 1981 and the struggle against Thatcherism were instructive to how the left should respond to today's crises. This article does not want to present a guise of political neutrality and certainly aligns itself more closely to the interpretation of the events as put forward by the left, but acknowledges that for political expediency, some of the more nuanced details of what occurred in August 2011 (and in 1981) may be shaped to fit the left's practical programme. As Smith (2010) has argued, riots and episodes of public unrest do not fall neatly into categories of political struggle and the motives and actions of those involved are open to a multitude of interpretations.

The Events of August 2011

The events of August 2011 began on August 6 when a gathering outside a police station in Tottenham, made up of local residents concerned over the shotting death of Mark Duggan during a police operation, transformed from a spontaneous assembly into a series of confrontations with the police. Over the Saturday of the 6th and throughout the following day, the disorder spread from Tottenham to other areas of North London, such as Wood Green and Enfield, then to other parts of the capital, including Hackney, Waltham Forest and Brixton. By Monday the 8th, most areas of London had experienced public unrest, with the "worst" experienced in Croydon, but major disturbances also occurred in Birmingham, Nottingham, Liverpool, as well as minor ones in Thames Valley, Bristol, Leeds and Huddersfield. On the fourth day, the riots had calmed down in London, but were still happening in Nottingham, Gloucester, Birmingham and Liverpool, and causing significant disorder in the Greater Manchester area, particularly Salford. As the *Reading the Riots* report by *The Guardian* and the London School of Economics (2011, p. 15) said:

> The riots began as small-scale disorder in Tottenham, north London, on 6 August. What began as a peaceful protest against the police shooting of a local black man, Mark Duggan, two days earlier, turned into more serious violence.

The cause, or causes, of the riots were much debated in the political sphere, in the press, on the internet and amongst the wider British population, with a myriad of differing reasons given for the outbreak of social unrest. Probably the most wide-ranging analysis of the riots conducted at this point, the

Reading the Riots report (2011, p. 4) concluded that there were several different reasons for the riots occurring. Firstly, the report found that "[w]idespread anger and frustration at people's every day treatment at the hands of the police was a significant factor in the summer riots in every major city where disorder took place", with the "focus of much resentment" amongst those that rioted being the "police use of stop and search, which was felt to be unfairly targeted and often undertaken in an aggressive and discourteous manner". The report (2011, p. 5) also noted that public outrage over Mark Duggan's death reverberated much further than Tottenham or its surrounding boroughs, stating that "[a]nger over the police shooting ... was repeatedly mentioned [by rioters] — even outside London". But alongside grievances directed towards the actions of the police, the report (2011, p. 5) noted that rioters also claimed another lot of motivating factors including "the increase of tuition fees", "the closure of youth services", "the scrapping of the education maintenance allowance" and broader "perceived social and economic injustices". The report (2011, p. 24), having interviewed 270 people from various backgrounds and lifestyles, said that "a great many shared, and talked animatedly about ... injustice and inequality", although this was expressed in many different ways, with the report arguing that "a pervasive sense of injustice" was "at [the] heart [of] what the rioters talked about". The report (2011, p. 24) talked about how this injustice was experienced and manifested in different ways:

> For some this was economic — the lack of a job, money or opportunity. For others it was more broadly social, not just the absence of material things, but how they felt they were treated compared with others ... Predictably these meant different things to different people, but the term that kept cropping up was "justice".

However, the interpretation of the reasons for the riots given by politicians and the police was less considered, with the consensus amongst the decision-making elites being that the riots were an outbreak of criminal violence and vandalism caused by a "broken Britain". In the first sitting on Parliament after the riots, David Cameron described the riots as "criminality, pure and simple", adding "there is absolutely no excuse for it" (House of Commons, *Hansard*, August 11, 2011, col. 1051) and it was not just the Conservatives who saw the riots as driven by criminal desire. In the same session of Parliament, Hazel Blears, the Labour MP for Salford and Eccles, said that the riots were "not about protest", but "about deliberate, organised, violent criminality" (House of Commons, *Hansard*, August 11, 2011, col. 1062).

In order to counter this argument that the riots of 2011 were somehow unique and unprecedented, several commentators and scholars have sought to put the most contemporary riots in a historical context, linking these riots to those that occurred in 1981, but also to other "moral panics" about youth, crime and public disorder in the urban environment. As Pearson (2012, p. 45) has written, "there is a long history of social anxiety that finds it crystallising focus in a preoccupation with the rising youth generation, and the crime and violence for which it is responsible". He further remarked that each time these social anxieties arose, such as during the 2011 riots, "they are accompanied by the same vocabulary of historically-illiterate complaints that are recycled as if they were new" (Pearson 2012, p. 61). Jefferson (2012, p. 8) wrote that any surprise expressed about the outbreak of the 2011 riots was "disingenuous" and argued that the "most surprising thing about this summer's riots was the surprise that greeted them; as if we had not seen their like before". Frost and Phillips (2012, p. 2.2) made a similar point, declaring that "the riots of 2011 are neither new or novel" and "riots more generally are not a new phenomenon and form an integral part of Britain's social and political landscape". Amongst those who proposed that the 2011 riots needed to be situated within a wider historical context, there were different suggestions of which historical narratives the riots fitted into. Jefferson (2012, p. 8) pointed to the riots of the late 1980s and 1990s, such as the poll tax riots, the riots in Cardiff, Tyneside and Oxford in 1991, the riots in the Asian areas of Manningham, Bradford, in 1995, as well as the disturbances which occurred in Bradford, Oldham and Burnley in 2001. Waddington (2012, p. 10) picked up on other, as well as some similar, episodes of public disorder:

> No one seemed to recall that only a few months earlier students had rioted and rampaged during protests against increased tuition fees. The G20 was already a distant memory along with the anti-capitalist rioting that stretched back to "J18" in 1999. Whilst the tenth anniversary of the riots of Burnley, Oldham and Bradford brought them to memory, their relevance escaped many. The inter-ethnic disorders in Lozells, Birmingham in 2007 seems to have been airbrushed out of the collective memory. Protests against the *Satanic Verses* might as well never have happened. Riots in Backbird Leys in Oxford, Ely in Cardiff, and on Tyneside in the early 1990s have been engulfed in the mists of time ...

Frost and Phillips (2012, p. 3.4) thought there "clear continuities in terms of perceived causal factors [used] to explain the historical outbreaks of riots and unrest", linking the discussion of riots of 2011 back to the "anti-black riots" of 1919 and 1948, which broke out in places such as Cardiff and Liverpool. Pearson (2012) evoked a narrative of "moral panic" about youth, crime and public unrest, which stretched from the "hooligans" of the urban slums in Victorian England to the "teds" and "rockers" of the 1950s and 1960s, then through to the "chavs" and "hoodies" of today. Hirschler (2012) put the most recent riots in the perspective of the "race riots" that occurred in Notting Hill in 1958 and the debate about "race" and immigration that occurred in the aftermath of both events.

But in all of the narratives and historical comparisons evoked in the aftermath of the 2011 riots, the spectre of the 1981 riots have proved central. It has become the benchmark against which nearly all facets of the most recent riots have been judged — in terms of causes of the riots, how the riots unfolded, the actions of those who rioted, communication during the riots, the response of the police, the political response and the post-riot debates. As said earlier in this article, historical contrast between the riots of 2011 and 1981 is warranted and necessary, but what has emerged from many discussions of the contrast between the two eras of riots is that the idea of "the 1981 riots" has been crystallised in different ways in the collective public memory and how the most recent riots are interpreted depends largely on how one interprets those that happened thirty years ago.

The Contested Causes of the 1981 Riots

In his book chapter on the historical context of the 2011 riots, Tim Bateman (2012, p. 95) argued that "[a]dequate time has elapsed since these earlier events [referring to 1981] to allow more objective explanatory accounts to emerge", but the passing of time also means that historical events become essentialised and the complexities of past events are more likely to be disregarded. Using George Rudé's idea of the rebellious crowd (described by Bateman as "a mechanism — frequently unconscious — by which dissent was expressed in a (largely) progressive direction"), he prescribes the 1981 riots as having a particular political identity, writing that the "[b]enefit of hindsight allows us to view the 1981 Brixton riots as fitting closely Rudé's account of the crowd" (Bateman 2012. p. 94, 104). However, it is the contention of this article that the causes of the 1981 riots, the motivations of those involved and the political nature of the riots have been highly contested.

As Smith (2010, p. 24) has argued, while agreeing that the 1981 riots had a political dimensions, both the (primarily white) British leftist groups and black activists tried to claim that the riots reflected their political outlook and historical lineages. The left predominantly saw the riots as the result of "widespread antipathy [felt] towards the socio-economic policies of the Conservative Government", while black activists and journalists "emphasised the role of black youth [in the unrest] and the racial discrimination and harassment experienced by the black communities that were integral factors in the outbreak of the rioting" (Smith 2010, p. 25). Smith (2010, p. 25) has written that "political positions ... cannot claim total possession of popular rebellion" and has used the work of Homi Bhabha to propose the "categorisation of popular struggle into one position ... negates the fact that the motives of all those involved are never identical". As Bhabha (1994, p. 26) has stated "our political referents and priorities ... are not there in some primordial, naturalistic sense. Nor do they reflect a unitary or homogeneous political object". As the history of various popular struggles and public unrest have shown, the objectives and intentions of those involved are "neither the one nor the other" and are always contested (Bhabha 1994, p. 26; Smith 2010, p. 25) In a similar vein, McDonald (2012, pp. 21-22) has talked about the existence of the "multiplicity of logics" at work in the collective, as well as individual, experiences of the riots, writing:

> it is not surprising that the riot does not possess a social or political project but is instead an embodied event in which the different logics at work appear to undermine each other and leave the participants in a situation captured by the masked man who says with such intensity: "I can't explain it".

Although much of the complexity seems to have been removed in contemporary discussion of the 1981 riots, there has been a consensus formed (quite rightly) that the riots that occurred in Brixton and then across the country had a discernable political element to them. As Frost and Phillips (2012, p. 1.1) wrote, the 1981 riots have been "viewed more sympathetically" than the 2011 events, "with meanings and grievances now largely understood and accepted, and even seen as noble". While the more recent riots "have been seen as lacking any real or legitimate grievances". Frost and Phillips (2012, p. 2.7) describe the 1981 riots as "highly politicised" and like many observers, see the disturbances of the 1980s as "politically grounded and motivated within particular oppressed communities", especially concerning the treatment of black youth by the police. By contrasting this identifiable anger at the racism of the police in the early 1980s with contemporary events, many commentators have created a dichotomy between the "legitimate" riots of 1981 and the "illegitimate" riots of 2011. Richardson (2011) has described this process:

> It was ... suggested that there is no comparison to be made with the riots of 1981 or other riots that have occurred since. It is apparently now accepted that those disturbances were sparked by genuine grievances, such as police brutality and racism. By contrast, the events this August were just looting: mad consumerism, feral youth, and a few selfish opportunists grabbing free stuff.

On the right-wing of politics, many seem to have taken a sympathetic (and liberal-left) reading of 1981 to make the contrast distinct with the 2011 riots. For example, O'Neill (2011) claimed that acts of apparent vandalism, such as "looting and the destruction of local infrastructure", were "largely incidental to the broader expression of political anger, by products of the main show, which was a clash between a community and the forces of the state". He further described the riots of the early 1980s as "politically motivated, anti-racist riots against the police" (O'Neill 2011). In contrast, O'Neill (2011) said that "in these new riots, smashing stuff up is all there is", arguing that the riots were "not a politically rebellion", but "a riotous expression of carelessness for one's own community". The Works and Pensions Secretary, Iain Duncan Smith, said on BBC's *Panorama* that "these riots were not riots like the ones of the 1980s", but "were intensely criminal activities" (cited in, Hughes 2011). Hughes (2011), writing for the *Morning Star*, quipped that this comment "made it sound like Duncan Smith was a bit of a fan of '80s riots, disappointed with today's version", stating that Duncan Smith was "trying to dismiss the social causes of today's riots by implying he and his kind accepted the social causes of yesterday's riots".

However, it was not just people to the right of centre that formed this argument, with similar points being made by some liberal-left commentators. In *The Independent*, columnist Hensher (2011) wrote that "[u]nlike the riots of thirty years ago, actions last week had no clear explanation" and that while the riots of 1981 "were the product of rage among the underclasses, the unemployed, the young whose future was in the process of being destroyed", the most recent riots "was all about shops". Wheatle (2011) said that while there was genuine dissatisfaction with the police and the Independent Police Complaints Commission, he did not "detect any resolve in the insurrectionists for them to take the police to account", unlike in 1981, when in Wheatle's words, "[w]e were battling for our voices to be finally heard and recognised by the institutions of this country who we believed hated our existence". Wheatle (2011) complained that in 2011 that "[t]here was no standing their ground making a lasting statement" and that he "couldn't identify any hint of political motive". Sivanandan (2011), the black activist and former editor of *Race & Class* journal, was interviewed by the *Socialist Worker* newspaper and while he acknowledged the socio-economic and political causes for the riots, he lamented:

> the rebellion is neither community-based nor politically-oriented — which is what distinguishes them from the disturbances of 1981 or 1985. Those were uprisings based on community organising. These are riots mobilised on a Blackberry.

What seemed to frustrate those on the liberal-left who made these sort of comments was the lack of an explicit political agenda of those involved in the 2011 riots, and that the riots seemed to differ from the 1981 blueprint. Lea and Hallsworth (2012, p. 30) wrote that the "concerns of the rioters have shifted from a clear response to manifest injustice ... to a more diffuse expression of generalised rage". And to these commentators, the lack of an explicit political agenda made it difficult to suggest practical and concrete solutions that might address the reasons for the outbreak of the riots. Hensher (2011) concluded:

> What the liberal was faced with in August was a frightening abyss: a catastrophic action motivated, perhaps, by the shallowest and least idealistic of desires; an action of destruction and selfishness which seemed, for a moment, universal rather than the motions of an angry — perhaps rightly angry — minority. What to do about that? No one had the faintest idea.

Thatcherism Repeating — the Lessons of the 1981 Riots as Resistance

While many scrambled to come up with a solution to the problems that caused the riots in August 2011, others already had a programme to deal with the apparent problems underlying the most recent disturbances. Amongst those with a ready-formed programme were the left-wing groups in the UK who saw the riots as a predictable reaction to the economic crisis and Conservative rule. All the left groups agreed that the riots were a response to the dire economic situation caused by decades of neoliberalism (with symptoms such as high youth unemployment, a lack of public spending in many urban areas and the emphasis upon consumerism) and exacerbated by the policies of the Cameron government, complemented with an overt "law and order" agenda by the criminal justice system that created hostilities between young people, including white and ethnic minority youth, and the police.

The official statement by the Socialist Workers Party (SWP 2011) stated that

> [t]his is what happens in a society of deep and growing inequality, where there are great pools of unemployment and poverty, where there is systematic police harassment and racism, and where many young people feel they have no future.

In the SWP's monthly magazine, *Socialist Review*, Richardson (2011) argued that "[t]he rage expressed on the streets of England in August is a legitimate expression of disgust against an unjust society". In the week after the riots, *The Socialist*, the newspaper of The Socialist Party of England and Wales (formerly Militant), ran an article written by a member of the Socialist Party's Executive Committee, which announced "we place the blame for what has taken place firmly on the Con-Dem government", arguing that the economic policies of the government and treatment of young people, particularly black youth, "as potential criminals" by the police were the two reasons for the riots (Belshon 2011, pp. 6-7). In another article, published in the Socialist Party's monthly magazine *Socialism Today*, a Party member wrote that:

> August's explosive events have exposed the reality of British capitalism: the enormous wealth gap, persistent racism, and the impact of the cuts, ... It has revealed a class society in crisis where all but the very rich are struggling and massive anger, boiling below the surface, can burst out at any time. (Sachs-Eldridge 2011)

In a speech at the Midlands District Congress of the Communist Party of Britain, an Executive Committee member listed a number of factors that were "a key backcloth" to the riots, which included:

> [t]he deepening economic crisis which is further re-distributing wealth for the top 10% whilst further impoverishing the other 90%, rising unemployment, growing disillusionment with the capitalist class and its state apparatus brought about by widely publicised evidence of endemic corruption ... , institutionalised racism, cuts to youth and other public services. (Stevenson 2011)

These factors were evidence, in his opinion, of the "sharpening contradictions within capitalism" and a resulting "ruling class offensive", which caused working class youth to be "swept up in ... a wave of sporadic, spontaneous and directionless displays of collective anger' (Stevenson 2011). As well as mentioning "round after round of spending cuts", the Communist Party of Great Britain's paper, the *Weekly Worker*, spoke of the "deeper causes" of the riots:

> Today's capitalist society is more and more focused on generating artificial needs and as a direct concomitant produces more and more alienation, hopelessness and despair. As the world of things expands, the world of people shrinks. Having hated school, being unemployed, or having a dead-end job, it is quite understandable why young people turn to petty criminality, hedonism and join street gangs. (Manson 2011, p. 8)

Another article in the *Weekly Worker* said, in discussion of this alienation of youth under neoliberal capitalism, "[n]o wonder then that rioting for some of them brought a moment of joy or release — even if it was only fleeting" (Ford 2011, p. 4). The Respect Party, led by George Galloway, called the riots the "predictable outcome to the enormous economic and social pressures [that] communities have been under as the Tory-led coalition government doles out its punishment to the poor and the working class", combined "with the tension that has long existed between the alienated youth of our inner cities and the police" (Wight 2011).

Within many of the analysis of the 2011 riots by groups and commentators on the organised left, reference was made to the riots of 1981 and was often held up as a blueprint for understanding what had occurred and what the next steps should be. Writing in the *Morning Star*, Czernik (2011) said that three factors had been present "[i]n every instance of violent urban unrest that has taken place in Britain since 1981", which were "an oppressive police presence, poverty and tensions arising from discrimination and deprivation". In his speech to the Midlands District Congress, CPB Executive Committee member Stevenson (2011) stated that the riots were "far from unique" and that "every period of capitalist economic crisis and an intensified class struggle has been punctuated with similar displays", claiming that "the wave of riots in the 1980s [occurred] in precisely the same working class areas" as the riots of 2011. Respect Party member Ovenden (2011) wrote on the Party's website that during the 2010 General Election, the Party's leader George Galloway warned:

> the last time the Tories came into replace an already dead Labour government and pursued full-blooded class war policies, Britain's cities went up in flames. That was 1981. Three decades later the Sunday supplement features on Brixton, Toxteth and St Paul's all situated those events in the aggressive policing, racist exclusion and darkening hopes of the young of the time ...
>
> They [the Conservatives] cannot accept that it is their policies, building on many more years of social polarisation and stigmatisation of the poorest that are the conditions which have produced today's riots.

However, the most detailed comparison between the events of 2011 and those of 1981 has been from the Socialist Workers Party, with much emphasis placed on the analysis of the 1981 riots by SWP thinker Harman (1981a; 1981b). One of the leading members of the SWP, Alex Callinicos posted online in the days following the riots that "[i]n its fundamentals, Chris Harman's classic analysis of the 1981 riots applies to what has been happening these last few days" (cited in, New Left Project 2011). The major analysis performed by members of the SWP, published in the Autumn 2011 issue of the Party's theoretical journal, *International Socialism*, heavily situated its understanding of what occurred in 2011 within Harman's characterisation of the 1981 riots, calling Harman's work "an indispensable text for understanding the dynamics of riots" (Jones 2011: fn 1) Jones (2011) used Harman's argument that under capitalism that the conditions for riots are preceded by two factors — "when strike action alone no longer seems enough to win workers' demands, or when sections of workers lose their faith in the ability of organisations based upon industrial action to achieve their goals" — and claimed that the riots of 2011 "clearly relate to both these instances" (Harman 1981b, cited in Jones 2011) The article further explained that when explicitly "political" outlets were out of reach of young people, "[t]he collective action embodied in rioting can be a liberating experience" (Jones 2011) and quoted Harman from 1981 to reinforce this point:

> Those without hope are capable suddenly, virtually out of nowhere, of shifting from apathy to anger. And that anger can break through all the restraints that education within capitalist society is supposed to build into people's consciousness. The local streets suddenly take on the aspect of a revolutionary battleground with barricades and burning cars and instant solidarity against the state. (Harman 1981a, cited in Jones 2011)

Another quote from Harman is also used to emphasise the political solidarity created by riots, claiming that

> riots, even more than strikes, provide people who have often lived desolate, atomised, boring lives with the experience of solidarity, of collective power, of being able to affect the course of society large instead of merely being on the receiving end

(Harman 1981b, cited in Jones 2011) The authority of Harman was also employed to emphasise the argument that "[w]hile rioters may not have a formulated list of demands, the riots were clearly a political act" (Jones 2011) and used Harman's writing as an example of this:

> [i]n 1981, ... there were almost no over politics in most of the big riots. They were spontaneous eruptions, led by those without worked-out political views, drawing behind them a cross-section of the youth in their areas. Yet the

experience of the riots will have been a very political one (Harman 1981(b)), cited in Jones 2011).

Using the insight provided by Harman, the article tells of how events initially perceived as "irrational outbursts of criminality at the time" have "later be seen as understandable events which have ... arisen from legitimate grievances and may have even had positive effects in the long term" (Jones 2011). By using Harman's analysis as the key to understanding previous riots, there is the assumption that the 2011 riots can be observed in the same way and that riots should be viewed as unconscious political manifestations of collective anger at the current political and economic system. This may very well be the case, but once again, the interpretation of the recent riots is viewed through the prism of 1981 and the politics are identified through (to use the term coined by Spivak (1988, p. 281) the "palimpsestic narrative" of the riots that occurred thirty years previously.

The answer to the riots, as well as to the wider political and economic situation that the UK has been facing, seems to be the same for the SWP today as it was in the early 1980s under Thatcher. The flyer produced by the Party in the aftermath of the riots spoke of organising demonstrations and strikes at venues such as the Conservative Party conference, claiming that "[s]uch struggles can unite desperate young people and workers who face job cuts, attacks on pensions, huge wage reductions and worsening conditions" (SWP 2011). The article on the riots in *International Socialism* called for socialists to intervene in the processes of revolt and engage with those involved in the riots and once again, used a quote from the 1980s (this time by Tony Cliff) to reinforce the message:

> The riots and looting have been fantastic, but they have not gone far enough. Because they have not been organised, the kids have attacked shops when they should have been attacking factories. We must teach them to take the bakery, not just the bread (Cliff, cited in Jones 2011).

Similar talk about linking up the organisations of the labour movement and youth has come from the Socialist Party (2011, p. 2), which has proposed that the "trade union movement needs to act to show it is on the side of young people" and has argued that for this proposed alliance to be "fully effective", it needs "to be linked to the struggle to develop a new mass party for workers and youth which stands for a socialist society". However, there is little discussion of how these leftist parties intend to practically broach the gap between the organised left and Britain's disaffected youth. It has been noted that the groups on the left that "might have traditionally provided focus for political frustration have ... witnessed varying levels of decline in the past thirty years" (Jones 2011) and if the lack of viable political options (or even a mistrust of politicians and politics in general) was a reason for the outbreak of the riots, it is difficult to see how the SWP, or any other political group on the left, will reverse this trend and reach out to those likely to get caught up in riotous events. It is worth noting that Cliff's proposed actions did not have much success in the fight against Thatcherism either and as Kenneth Roberts has argued, in the aftermath of the 1981 riots, "[r]ather than being channelled into party politics", a large number of young people remained apolitical and "their discontents [were] more likely expressed on the streets" (Roberts 1984, p. 182).

Diverging Entry Points in the Grand Narrative

As mentioned earlier in this article, different commentators on the 2011 riots have attempted to place these events into a wider historical context, although the historical narratives in which the riots of 2011 have been situated have varied, often depending on the political arguments being made. This article has argued that the 1981 riots have been a focal point for narratives that link the riots of today with the riots of yesteryear, but these are not the only two time periods located on many of the narratives evoked. Because of the locations in which the riots first occurred, Broadwater Farm in Tottenham, and their spread to Birmingham, particularly the area of Handsworth, there has been considerable attention paid to the riots of 1985, but the 1985 riots are often combined with those of 1981 as the "justifiable" riots of the early Thatcher years. The same, to a lesser extent, has happened in relation to discussing the riot in the St Paul's district of Bristol, which occurred in April 1980 and is often seen a precursor to the Brixton riots the following year. While some have explored the possible connections between the events in Bristol in 1980 and the 2011 riots (Clement 2012), in the minds of many who have discussed the narratives of the riots, the disturbances that transpired over a five-year period in the 1980s have become amalgamated in many ways as the Bristol-Brixton/Toxteth/Mosside-Broadwater Farm/Handsworth riots, even though the disturbances that occurred across these areas and across the years were quite varied in context, direct causes, what happened, the response by the authorities and outcomes.

With an emphasis on understanding the political dimensions of the riots, it has been commentators on the left who have sought to place the latest riots in a historical context, often linking the most recent events to other episodes of popular dissent and revolt by the lower classes. The Socialist Party linked the riots to the unemployment struggles that occurred in Birkenhead in 1932 (Belshon 2011, p. 6) and the strikes that broke out across the UK in 1911 (colloquially known as the "Great Unrest"), with two articles printed in *The Socialist* in the week following the 2011 riots (Palmer 2011, p. 11; Mulhearn 2011, p. 11). Former leading SWP members (now part of a group called Counterfire) Rees and German (2011) linked the riots back to the Peasants' Revolt of 1381, the Gordon Riots of 1780 and the unemployed struggles of 1886-87 (also mentioned by Harman 1981b, pp. 15-16) in his analysis). The Socialist Party was keen to make connections between the riots as a form of popular dissent and the 1990 anti-poll tax demonstrations, as its former incarnation, Militant, were heavily involved in the fight against the Poll Tax, arguing that this "chaotic and inchoate expression of protest" needed to be directed more towards a strategy of "mass, organised "law-breaking", which had characterised the anti-poll tax campaign (Sachs-Eldridge 2011). For the Socialist Party, the victory was not necessarily the massive anti-poll tax demonstration-cum-riot of March 1990, but "achieved through organising democratic local, regional and national anti-poll tax federations that painstakingly built confidence in the tactic of non-payment" (Sachs-Eldridge 2011). From more recent times, the Socialist Workers Party put forward that the protests against higher education tuition fees that arose in late 2010 and early 2011 and the August riots were both manifestations of the anger of British youth against the current political and economic climate, with Jones (2011) writing:

> [t]he involvement of large numbers of young working class people in the student movement, with its accompanying destruction of symbols of authority, alongside the experience of harassment from the police, may have made participation in riots a natural evolution.

The process of placing the events of 2011 within a wider narrative that spans (at least) back to 1981 has the potential to alter perceptions of the riots that happened in the 1980s, with certain elements of these episodes of public disorder highlighted to construe some form of continuity. This process can obliterate the fact that, at the time, the riots of the early 1980s were seen as part of other historical narratives — older narratives which are erased by more recent ones. Many black activists, journalists and commentators, as seen in the reactions to the 1981 riots published in *Race & Class* and *Race Today* (Author unknown 1981; CARF Collective 1981; Howe 1982; see Smith 2010), portrayed these widespread disturbances in a longer historical narrative of black resistance to police harassment and racial violence. Different starting points were mentioned, such as the riots that broke out after the murder of Charles Wootton in Liverpool in 1919, the Notting Hill riots of 1958 and the community response after the police raids on Notting Hill's Mangrove Restaurant in 1969-1970. Sivanandan (1982, p. 3) even suggested that the starting point of these modern struggles by black Britons did not begin in the UK, but were formed in the anti-colonial struggles within the British Empire, with Sivanandan's narrative black rebellion in Britain beginning with the hanging of Udham Singh, who shot dead Sir Michael O'Dwyer in London for his leadership during a massacre of unarmed peasants and workers in Amritsar in 1919. This long narrative accelerated in the mid-1970s, with the narrative going from the disorder at the Notting Hill Carnival in August 1976 to the anti-National Front demonstration at Southall in April 1979, then the riot in Bristol in 1980, then the Brixton riots in April 1981 and ending with the riots across Britain in July of the same year. As the journal *Race & Class* reported, "[i]n many ways what happened during and after the 1976 carnival was a premonition of the later 'riots'" (author unknown 1981, p. 239). A specific example of how one event influenced another was mentioned: "St Pauls became a symbol of resistance — black youths chanted "Bristol, Bristol, Bristol" at police defending a National Front March in Lewisham, South London, later the same month" (author unknown 1981, p. 223).

It is interesting to note that these episodes of black rebellion, that loomed large in the consciousness when the 1981 riots first occurred and were discussed, have not been evoked in the same way in discussions of the 2011 riots. One possible reason for this despite clashes between the police and Britain's ethnic minority communities being one of the reasons for the August 2011 riots, these events have not been claimed as episodes of "black" rebellion and have been more collectively regarded as an example of wider lower class anger — what Lea and Hallsworth (2012, p. 31) described as "a diffuse and generalised rage of a dispossessed population angry at a system that has failed them but with no vision of an alternative" (also see Frost & Phillips 2012, pp. 2.4-2.8). An article in *The Guardian* by three of the authors of the *Reading the Riots* report quoted a community leader in Brixton as saying, "[t]he riots that took place in August were not about race but about a growing underclass in our inner cities that feels excluded, isolated and locked out of mainstream society" (Newburn, Lewis & Metcalf 2011). The same article also interviewed another Brixton youth worker, who argued that "what has really changed in the past thirty years is that, while many young black people continue to feel the same way as his generation had in 1981, "now that feeling is shared by white working-class people" (Newburn, Lewis & Metcalf 2011).

Conclusion

Power (2011) wrote in *The Guardian* after the initial burst of public disorder in North London last year that "[i]mages of burning buildings, cars aflame and stripped-out shops may provide spectacular fodder for a restless media ... but we will understand nothing of these events if we ignore the history and the context in which they occur". This article has looked at how different commentators, journalists, politicians, scholars and activists have interpreted the historical context of the riots that happened across the UK in August 2011, particularly focusing on how the most recent riots have been seen through the lens of the riots from 1981. Although providing a historical background to the 2011 riots helps us to understand that these riots did not occur from out of nowhere or that they were unprecedented in any way, but the comparison of the two events has, in many ways, crystallised how the 1981 riots are perceived in the collective memory. Notions of what "the 1981 riots" or "the Brixton riots" or "the Toxteth riots" have come to symbolise are essentialised ideas of the "noble" or "justified" riots against institutional racism and Thatcherism — in other words, the events of 1981 were explicitly *political*.

This article has argued that framing the 1981 riots in this way has had two effects on how the 2011 riots are perceived. Firstly, commentators, journalists and politicians on the right (as well as some on the liberal-left) have used the idea of the 1981 riots as expressions of political frustration against "legitimate" targets to condemn the criminal and destructive activities of the rioters involved in the unrest in 2011, arguing that those involved in the most recent riots were motivated by consumerist desire and anti-social behaviour and thus, the response by the authorities should be criminal justice oriented, rather than making political concessions. Secondly, commentator and activists on the left have taken the framework of the 1981 riots as explicitly political actions from the lower classes to show that the riots of 2011 were just as political and represented the anger of the growing "underclass" in the UK. For many on the left and within activist circles, the same neoliberal/monetarist agenda by the Conservatives (resulting in high unemployment and cuts to public services), combined with the institutional racism of the police and the judiciary, were the underlying causes of the riots of 2011 and those that occurred in the early 1980s, and that the lessons of the battles against the Thatcher government are to be heeded.

However, this essentialised version of the 1981 riots, and the comparison with contemporary events, overlooks the fact that the riots that broke out across Britain thirty years ago were not as neat to categorise and interpret as they look in hindsight, and that at the time, there were clear differences in how the riots were understood by different sections of society. Even for those that agreed that the riots were political disagreed on whether the riots were a response by the lower classes to socio-economic policies of the Thatcher government or a response by the black communities to the racism that they faced in Britain on a day-to-day basis. The evoking of the riots of 1981 in the discourse on the August 2011 riots has been used by commentators from both sides of politics to portray the most recent riots in a particular manner, using the supposed explicit political nature of the riots of the past to dismiss or emphasise the political nature of the riots of the present. While historical comparisons are useful for understanding the wider context of events, such as the public unrest of 2011, in too many scenarios, the past is distorted and simplified to fit the political demands of the present.

References

Author unknown (1981) 'The Riots', *Race & Class*, vol. 23, nos. 2-3, pp. 223-232.

Bateman, T. (2012) 'With the Benefit of Hindsight: The Disturbances of August 2011 in Historical Context', in Briggs, D. (ed.), *The English Riots of 2011: The Summer of Discontent*, Waterside Press, Sherfield Gables, pp. 91-109.

Belshon, J. (2011) Con-Dems to Blame for Anger of Youth, *The Socialist*, no. 64, August 18-31, pp. 6-7.

Bhabha, H. (1994) *The Location of Culture*, Routledge, London.

Collective, C. A. R. F. (1981) 'Background: British Racism', *Race & Class*, vol. 23, no. 2-3, pp. 232-244.

Clement, M. (2012) 'Rage Against the Market: Bristol's Tesco Riot', *Race & Class*, vol. 53, no. 3, pp. 81-90.

Czernik, A. (2011) Broken Britain: Broken Record, *Morning Star Online*, August 16, http://www.morningstaronline.co.uk/news/content/view/full/108345 (accessed 26 September 2012).

Ford, E. (2011) Aftermath of August, *Weekly Worker*, no. 879, September 1, p. 4.

Frost, D. & Phillips, R. (2012) The 2011 Summer Riots: Learning From History — Remembering 81, *Sociological Research Online*, 17/3, http://www.socresonline.org.uk/17/3/19.html (.accessed 18 September 2012).

Gilroy, P. (2011) Paul Gilroy Speaks on the Riots, August 2011, Tottenham, North London, *The Dreams of Safety*, August 16, http://dreamofsafety.blogspot.com.au/2011/08/paul-gilroy-speaks-on-riots-august-2011.html (accessed 26 September 2012).

The Guardian/LSE (2011) *Reading the Riots: Investigating England's Summer of Disorder*, The Guardian, London.

Harman, C. (1981a) From riot to revolution, *Socialist Review*, vol. 1, no. 5, May, http://www.marxists.org/archive/harman/1981/05/riotrev.htm (accessed 1 November 2012).

Harman, C. (1981b) The summer of 1981: A Post-Riot Analysis, *International Socialism*, vol. 2, no. 14, Autumn, pp. 1-43.

Hensher, P. (2011) 'I'm a Bleeding-Heart Liberal — so, What am I to Make of These Sickening Scenes', *The Independent* (online), August 14, http://www.independent.co.uk/voices/commentators/philip-hensher/philip-hensher-im-a-bleedingheart-liberal--so-what-am-i-to-make-of-these-sickening-scenes-2337148.html (accessed 18 October 2012).

Hirschler, S. (2012) 'Riots in retrospective: Immigration and the crisis of the "other"', in Briggs, D. (ed.), *The English Riots of 2011: The summer of discontent*, Waterside Press, Sherfield Gables, pp. 65-88.

Howe, D. (1982) Brixton Before the Uprising, *Race Today*, February/March, pp. 62-64

Hughes, S. (2011) Tory Rewriting doesn't Wash, *Morning Star Online*, August 18, http://www.morningstaronline.co.uk/index.php/news/content/view/full/108434 (accessed 26 September 2012).

Jefferson, T. (2012) 'Policing the Riots: From Bristol and Brixton to Tottenham, via Toxteth Handsworth, etc.', *Criminal Justice Matters*, vol. 87, no. 1, pp. 8-9.

Jones, J. (2011) August 2011: A Riot of Our Own, *International Socialism*, vol. 2, no. 132, October, http://www.isj.org.uk/?id=758 (accessed on 24 September, 2012).

Lea, J. & Hallsworth, S. (2012) 'Understanding the Riots', *Criminal Justice Matters*, vol. 87, no. 1, pp. 30-31.

Manson, P. (2011) A fleeting moment of power, pure joy and fulfilment, *Weekly Worker*, no. 878, August 11, p. 8.

Marx, K. (1969) *The Eighteenth Brumaire of Louis Bonaparte*, International Publishers, New York, NY.

McDonald, K. (2012) 'They can't do nothing' to us today', *Thesis Eleven*, vol. 109, no. 1, pp. 17-23.

McSmith, A. (2011) Any Politically Embarrassing Findings can Just be Ignored', *The Independent* (online version), August 17, http://www.independent.co.uk/voices/commentators/andy-mcsmith-any-politically-embarrassing-findings-can-just-be-ignored-2338859.html (accessed 11 October 2012).

Mulhearn, T. (2011) Liverpool 1911 – Jack's story, *The Socialist*, no. 64, August 18-31, p. 11.

Newburn, T, Lewis, P. & Metcalf, J. (2011) A new kind of riot? From Brixton 1981 to Tottenham 2011, *The Guardian Online*, December 9, http://www.guardian.co.uk/uk/2011/dec/09/riots-1981–2011-differences (accessed 24 September 2012)

New Left Project. (2011) Left Groups Respond to the Riots, *NLP Blog*, August 10, http://www.newleftproject.org/index.php/site/blog_comments/left_groups_respond_to_the_riots (accessed 31 October 2012).

O'Neill, B. (2011) London's Burning: A Mob Made by the Welfare State, *Spiked Online*, August 9, http://www.spiked-online.com/site/printable/10970 (accessed 18 October 2012).

Ovenden, K. (2011) Mama said, they'll de days like this, *Respect Party Website*, August 15, http://www.respectparty.org.uk/2011/08/mama-said-they'll-be-days-like-this.html (accessed 30 October 2012).

Palmer, J. 'The Great Unrest 2011: When the Press Raged About "mob rule"', *The Socialist*, no. 64, August 18-31, p. 11.

Pearson, G. (2012) 'Everything Changes, Nothing Moves: The Longue Durée of Social Anxieties About Youth Crime', in Briggs, D. (ed.) *The English Riots of 2011: The Summer of Discontent*, Waterside Press, Sherfield Gables, pp. 45-63.

Power, N. (2011) There is a Context to London's Riots That Can't be Ignored, *The Guardian Online*, August 8, http://www.guardian.co.uk/commentisfree/2011/aug/08/context-london-riots (accessed 2 November 2012).

Rees, J. & German, L. (2011) A Short History of the London Riot, Counterfire Website, August 9, http://www.counterfire.org/index.php/articles/75-our-history/14476–a-short-history-of-the-london-riot (accessed November 2, 2012).

Richardson, B. (2011) After the riots, *Socialist Review*, September, http://www.socialistreview.org.uk/article.php?articlenumber=11747 (accessed 31 October 2012).

Roberts, K. (1984) Youth Unemployment and Urban Unrest, in Benyon, J. (ed.), *Scarman and After: Essays Reflecting on Lord Scarman's Report, the Riots and their Aftermath*, Pergamon Press, Oxford.

Sachs-Eldridge, S. (2011) Who Broke Britain? *Socialism Today*, September, http://www.socialismtoday.org/151/riots.html (accessed 30 October 2012).

Sivanandan, A. (1982) *A Different Hunger: Writings on Black Resistance*, Pluto Press, London.

Sivanandan, A. (2011) This is not the end of rebellion – it is the beginning, *Socialist Worker* (online), August 20, www.socialistworker.co.uk/art.php?id=25716 (accessed 24 September 2012).

Smith, E. (2010) 'Conflicting Narratives of Black Youth Rebellion in Modern Britain', *Ethnicity and Race in a Changing World: A Review Journal*, vol. 1, no. 3, pp. 16-32.

Socialist Party. (2011) A mass workers' movement is needed to defeat this rotten government, *The Socialist*, no. 64, August 18–31, p. 2.

Spivak, G. (1988) 'Can the Subaltern Speak?', in Nelson, C. & Grossberg, L. (eds) *Marxism and the Interpretation of Culture*, University of Illinois Press, Urbana, pp. 271-313.

Stevenson, B. (2011) CP Executive Committee speech to Midlands District Congress, http://www.communist-party.org.uk/index.php?view=article&catid=142%3Aengland&id=1397%3Amidlands-district-congress-2011-ben-stevenson-cp-executive-speech&tmpl=component&print=1&layout=default&page=&option=com_content&Itemid=202 (accessed 31 October 2012).

SWP. (2011) Police Brutality and Tory Attacks Caused the Riots, *SWP flyer*, http://www.socialistworker.co.uk/graphics/2011/keep/swstatementforweb.pdf (accessed 31 October 2012)

Vulliamy, E. (2011) Toxteth Revisited, 30 Years After the Riots, *The Observer Online*, July 3, http://www.guardian.co.uk/uk/2011/jul/03/toxteth-liverpool-riots-30-years.

Waddington, P. (2012) 'Explaining the Riots', *Criminal Justice Matters*, vol. 87, no. 1, pp. 10-11.

Walker, P. (2011) Brixton: Could it happen again? 30 years after the riots, *The Guardian Online*, April 2, http;//www.guardian.co.uk/theguardian/2011/apr/02/brixton-riots-anniversary

Wheatle, A. (2011) Tottenham 2011 and Brixton 1981 — different ideals, similar lessons, *The Guardian Online*, August 9, http://www.guardian.co.uk/commentisfree/2011/aug/09/tottenham-2011-brixton-1981 (accessed 1 October 2012)

Wight, J. (2011) Riots and Condemnation Without Context, RESPECT Party Website, August 10, http://www.respectparty.org/2011/08/riots-and-condemantion-without-context.html (accessed 30 October, 2012)

From Cairo to Tottenham: Big Societies, Neoliberal States, Colonial Utopias

Caroline Rooney

While the August riots are quite readily understood as an outburst provoked by the negligence of the neoliberal state, there has been a widespread failure amongst Western commentators and politicians to understand the extent to which the Egyptian revolution should also be understood as an uprising against neoliberalism. This essay draws on cultural sources, journalism and socio-economic analyses to make the case that Mubarak's Egypt could be understood in terms of neoliberal forms of the Big Society, especially, that of the gated community. In demonstrating the reliance of the neoliberal state on security policies based on policing, the essay goes on to analyse the riots in such terms. Even as the Egyptian revolution and the riots shared similar sources of frustration, their quite different manifestations are explained in terms of differing structures of feeling, those of dignity and pride. Finally, a postcolonial framework of analysis is brought to bear on the material considered by the essay to show the persistence of the colonial structures of neoliberal capitalism.

The Big Society demands mass engagement: a broad culture of responsibility, mutuality and obligation. But how do we bring this about? David Cameron.
(*The Big Society Debate*, p. 7)

Breaking News: President Mubarak was seen holding a big banner that read: "The president demands the change of the people."
(*Translating Egypt's Revolution*, p. 201)

The August riots of 2011 may be said to have exposed the contradictions and failures entailed in the advocacy of the Big Society, the flagship policy of the current British Government. As will be argued, this is because the formula of the Big Society presents itself as a "policy" without policies, as well as a call for engagement on the basis of disengagement, a dilemma which has begged the question of what the term "Big Society" actually refers to. In "'Big Society' as a rhetorical intervention," Martin Albrow writes: "when the meaning of 'Big Society' arose in a discussion among senior officials they received the authoritative response, 'Don't try to define it. It's meant to be mushy'" (p. 111).

This article proposes to juxtapose an analysis of the Egyptian revolution as an outcome of big society ideology with an analysis of the August riots: surprisingly so, in that Mubarak's Egypt has not been identified in terms of this ideology, and revolution not usually considered as its possibly logical implication. The aim of this comparative approach is to demonstrate the dissociation of Big Society rhetoric from social realities, as well as to confront the question of what a big society might actually mean in reality.[1]

In what follows, sociopolitical analysis will be combined with literary analysis for a number of reasons. What the Egyptian revolution and other uprisings over the course of 2011 have demonstrated is that protest movements express themselves through the cultural and aesthetic forms of the popular imagination. This is firstly a matter of a Benjaminian affirmation of how the democratization of art forms enables a critique of ideological mystifications, where Benjamin's perspective may be said to have proved more pertinent than Adorno's dismissal of popular culture as inevitably commodified (Benjamin 1969; Adorno 2007). Secondly, it is worth noting that when writers take on the role of communal scribe in conditions of social upheaval, the literary material in question is able to afford insights into popular consciousness that may be unavailable elsewhere. For instance, North African writers and literary texts have served strikingly to predict the Arab Spring through attending to what Area Studies specialists were failing to notice (Rooney 2011b). Regarding this, there are two particular points to note. The first is that liberation literature tends to have a prospective as opposed to retrospective outlook. The second is that an engagement with literary and cultural sources enables attention to be paid to subjective and affective structures that are also modes of mobilization, as this article will come to explain through attending to languages of pride and dignity.

Flash Points: Turning a Blind Eye

What the Tunisian and Egyptian uprisings and the London riots particularly had in common is that they were sparked by individual deaths that provoked widespread outrage for similar underlying reasons, even though the circumstances of each of the deaths differ. This identification of a certain commonality of the flash point, or tipping point, pertains also to other riots, as Diane Abbot comments of earlier race riots: "Starts with a black person dying at the hands of the police, Cherry Groce, Mrs Jarrett" (Slovo 2011, p. 35).

It may be said that the martyrdom of Mohamed Bouazizi in Sidi Bou Zid, the killing of Khaled Said in Alexandria and the killing of Mark Duggan in Tottenham, respectively, provoked a shared sense of deep affront in each situation over the lack of value accorded to the lives of ordinary people by

---

1. In this article, I use capitals for the policy (Big Society), and lower case for the phenomenon (big society), while the latter is more accurately a case of civil society.

those in power. Asmaa Mafhouz in her, now, famous vlog stated the following: "Four Egyptians set themselves on fire hoping the Tunisian revolution could be replicated; hoping Egypt could be a free country, where they could live in justice, have dignity, and be treated as human beings" (Mehrez, p. 76).

In the three iconic cases referred to above, it is not that the individual men were merely seen as innocent victims by those moved to protest their deaths. Rather than ascertaining complete innocence or degrees of criminality in individual cases, what is pertinent to understanding the social fault lines is the automatic criminalization or demonization, and thereby *shunning*, of a whole class of people. The fact that the flash points of the social unrest and uprisings were not anticipated indicates that they could be construed as blind spots that are, in fact, better understood in terms of "turning a blind eye" to certain conditions of exclusion. As such, the situation concerns the performative structuring of societies on the basis of an assimilationist/outcast logic, a categorical imposition that aims to determine reality while it is one that is divorced from the reality it purports to represent. The performativity in question may be said to be that of neoliberal capitalism.

The formula of the Big Society, as a government directive, is one that clearly serves the dictates of neoliberalism. Economist Ha-Joon Chang notes that free-market economists recommend: "the portion of the economy controlled by politicians and bureaucrats should be minimized." He adds: "Deregulation and privatization, in this view, are not only economically efficient but also politically sensible in that they minimize the very possibility that public officials can use the state as a vehicle to promote their own self-interests, at the cost of the general public" (p. 45). This prescription begs both the question of how those disempowered — rather than empowered — by deregulation and privatization are able to contest this state of affairs, and the question of how the self-interests of public officials may actually be aligned with the free market as opposed to at odds with it. In spite of this, the Big Society ideology advocates "social responsibility, not state control", (Cameron 2010) which in effect means diminished social responsibility on the part of the state. Szreter and Ishkanian write in their introduction to *The Big Society Debate*: "Hilton's research indicates that in Britain since the 1970s its activist and participatory citizenry have become increasingly disenchanted, not with their own 'broken society', but with an increasingly broken state, which no longer provides the facilitating framework" (p. 17).

The Gated Community Big Society or Mubarak's *Mukhabarat*

To speak of "the gated community big society" is a contradiction in terms, which is precisely my point. What has been insufficiently grasped is how Egypt under Mubarak functioned simultaneously as a gated community and as a big society (in neoliberal terms). A postcolonial analysis is helpful in establishing the nature of such a paradox.

In *Wretched of the Earth* (1961), Fanon's concern as regards new postcolonial nations is that the parties assuming power seem likely to shrink the national struggle to the interests of elites, as based not only on class but also on religion and on ethnic groups. In addition, Fanon considered that this turn towards a nepotistic style of politics to be a matter of the inability of the elite class to run their countries. In brief, lacking the policies for effective development, the elite are left with the aim of merely keeping themselves in power, through protecting their own wealth and through enacting but a facade of governance. The dictatorships in question are not dictatorships of ideologically driven totalitarian control and invasiveness. Rather, the people are abandoned. Reliance on the army on the part of the ruling class arises through just trying to maintain this state of affairs against any objection to it. In a Middle Eastern context, this is a case of the *mukhabarat* or security state.

Mubarak should be considered as the kind of weakly ineffectual dictator foreseen by Fanon, as opposed to an all-controlling totalitarian type of dictator. The experience of Cairo prior to the revolution was one of an anarchic society, in certain respects a leaderless one, in that the government lacked any effective policies and the people were thus left to fend for themselves in any way they could.[2] For example, there were no policies to tackle large-scale unemployment, and so the difficulty in making a living necessitated demeaning ways of coping — such as resorting to prostitution for tourists (Bradley, p. 160) — and proved conducive to scams and widespread corruption, together with the corruption of the "fat cats" out for themselves. When I interviewed novelist Khaled Al Khamissi in 2010, he quipped that Egyptians would not necessarily mind a dictatorship if it were a dictatorship that actually worked, that is, to improve conditions for ordinary people (See Rooney 2011).

In keeping with the above, contemporary Egyptian literature over the last decade presents us with scathing portrayals of a society that is uncohesive, untrustworthy and uncaring: for example, Ahmed Alaidy's *Being Abbas El Abd*, Ahmed Towfik's *Utopia* and Alaa Al Aswany's *The Yacoubian Building* (see Rooney 2009, 2013; Sakr forthcoming). Journalist John Bradley describes the Cairo milieu depicted in *The Yacoubian Building* in the following terms:

> The rich in this portrayal of Egypt get ever richer, and the poor ever poorer […] Radical Islamists prey on the vulnerable and the destitute *abandoned by the system*. The urbane and educated are trampled underfoot by mafia-like thugs known in Arabic as the "war rich" — better translated into English as "fat cats." (my emphasis, p. 2)

Bradley's book, published in 2008, is entitled *Inside Egypt: The Land of the Pharaohs on the Brink of a Revolution*. Based on conversations with a range of Egyptians, and notably influenced by the literary analyses of Al Aswany, it is the only book by a foreign journalist that I am aware of that predicted the co-

2. This is what I discovered when based in Cairo, 2009–2010.

ming revolution, where Bradley concludes his study by stating that Egypt is "ripe" for one of its periodic uprisings (p. 221). In his book, Bradley stresses the sheer incompetence of Mubarak's government as follows:

> The truly awful thing about the Mubarak regime is just how bankrupt it is, as it muddles aimlessly along. There is no ideological rationale that it offers, no standards to which the people can be rallied [...]

> The regime's political party has no real links to the people, and outside the major cities is barely a presence. In short, Mubarak's regime has none of the attributes that kept either the Soviets or the Chinese Communist parties in power. It has no reason for being, other than to cling to power. In the absence of any kind of legitimacy, what keeps it in power is therefore fear. (p. 213)

While such a state becomes a security state, relying on security services that haphazardly imprison and torture dissenters, the paradox is that this practice of intimidation coexists with a society that is in many other respects left entirely to its own devices. What accompanies this kind of Big Society is what may be termed the gated community phenomenon of the elites. Seeking to screen out the chaos around them, the rich elites in Egypt retreated increasingly into gated community worlds, escaping the city and any responsibility for it. Egyptian sociologist Mona Abaza writes: "First, the rich have opted to move out of the centre of Cairo, to the outskirts, to new satellite cities on the eastern and western parts of the Egyptian desert [...] Second, the zone of the Nile Corniche [...] nicknamed by several investors the 'Bermuda triangle', has witnessed a process of the 'cleaning-up' of popular life" (p. 1075). Timothy Mitchell comments that the private development tracts of Greater Cairo in the 1990s (with names such as Dreamland and Utopia) "represented the largest real-estate explosion Cairo had ever seen" (p. 2).

Ahmed Towfik's novel, *Utopia*, which appeared in 2008, constitutes a biting satire of the striking divorce of the "fat cat" world from that of the poor, where as Bradley correctly observes, Egypt has little in the way of a middle class as an alternative to these extremes. *Utopia*, obviously a dystopian mock-futuristic tale (set in 2023), establishes its *mise-en-scène* as follows:

> At the beginning of the twenty-first century, in the last census to be held, there were thirty-five million Egyptians living below the poverty line [...] A society without a middle class is primed for explosion.

> That is exactly what happened, but the explosion did not do away with the wealthy class. It decimated what remained of the middle class, and turned society into two poles and two peoples.

> Only the wealthy class realized that there was no life for it unless it became completely isolated, following the same logic behind medieval castles, when rulers would hold decadent parties while pestilence dominated the sea of poverty outside. (p. 108)

The novel is mainly narrated by a first person narrator who belongs to the "utopian" gated community class, although the authorial narrator, Towfik, introduces an ironic consciousness into the narration throughout, by means of his use of dramatic monologue techniques. The consumerist world of luxury in the novel is presented as one of utter boredom, as the following quotation shows:

> What can you do in this artificial paradise? You sleep, you take drugs, you eat until food makes you sick, you vomit until you can recover the enjoyment of eating, you have sex (it's wierd that you notice how boredom makes your sexual behaviour aggressive and sadistic). If you knew another way for a person to live his life, I'd be happy if you could tell me about it. (p. 9)

In this golden ghetto, the young take to relieving their boredom through two means: through taking an ecstacy drug called "phlogistine" and through the forbidden adrenalin sport of hunting. Hunting, it turns out, is a trophy sport and consists of forays into the jungle of the poor to kill one of them for display. The narrator sets off on such a trip, which takes him into the filthy suburbs of destitution where he encounters thugs, pimps and prostitutes; a world where rape is common and the people eat dog meat. The novel certainly does not romanticize the underclasses and the narrator's descent into the underworld does not lead to a humanizing vision. Rather, in a section narrated by its underclass protagonist, the novel advances the following analysis (which is overlaid with authorial allegory): "The Egyptian character has suffered a lot of damage in the last hundred years; it's like a wife whose husband treated her brutally for several years until she ended up closer to brutishness and viciousness" (p. 103).

In spite of its bleak nihilism, *Utopia* introduces us to characters amongst the poor in whom the reader is able to find some unexpected altruism and decency. The narrator, on being captured by a gang, encounters a man called Gaber, a name that could derive from the Arabic for "force" or for "assistance" (while Shafiq Gabr is, ironically, the name of an Egyptian billionaire property developer), who is willing to help him find his way back to Utopia. The narrator is untouched by this charitable act, raping Gaber's sister and killing Gaber as his trophy before he makes it back home. The novel ends prophetically (first appearing in 2009), with the poor beginning to rise up, attacking the "biroil" (synthetic oil) convoys of the rich and marching on their gated communities (see Sakr forthcoming). We are left with the image of the narrator trying to gun them down, strikingly depicted in the language of settler colonialism:

> This was my land and this was my world. I was born here. If my father stole these rights, then they had become my birthright, and I wouldn't give them up for the likes of Gaber, beggars and street whores [...] I wrenched the machine gun from the hands of a Marine [American] standing beside me, and aimed it at the mass of humanity advancing on the horizon. (pp. 155-156)

For the purposes of this analysis, what is interesting about the novel's satire of Egyptian society is its stark depiction of two worlds that have nothing to do with each other so that it would not be possible to say that they made up a nation state: the state disunited in the manner of settler colonialism. On the one hand, there is the self-sufficiency of the Utopian community that is built to screen out the underclass and on the other hand there is the underclass left to resort to criminality just to keep alive. While some members of the underclass are employed as servants in Utopia, the majority of members appear unemployed, organizing themselves into criminal gangs and thug squads. Regarding this extreme dissociation of worlds, the implication of the novel is that capitalism, especially neoliberal capitalism, overrides national boundaries in creating new boundaries that consist of miniature states or internal *colonies* of privilege with their security fences, but where these mini-states are networked with each other by means of international capital and military connections. In fact, Egyptian gated communities sport names that not only reflect dreams and fantasies but also reflect cosmopolitan or trans-metropolitan aspirations: for example, there are developments named Beverly Hills and Hyde Park. David Harvey writes: "It never did make much sense to speak of a distinctively US vs. British or French or German or Korean capitalist class. The international links were always important, particularly through colonial and neocolonial activities", and he adds that neoliberalism has intensified this kind of connectivity (p. 35). At the outset of Towfik's novel, the narrator states:

> Sixteen years old, and you don't belong anywhere except Utopia. You're a Utopian resident, softened by a life of luxury and boredom. You end up unable to tell an American from an Egyptian from an Israeli. (p. 6)

His friends in Utopia are indeed American Marines and Israelis. What this obviously alludes to is the way in which Mubarak maintained his power through American aid money, two billion a year, the second biggest sum of aid donation by America after its aid to Israel. America's aid money served as a bribe to keep Mubarak on the side of Israel, something he managed with difficulty given the overwhelming sympathy for Palestine in Egypt (Al Aswany 2011, p. 19). In addition, this aid money was tied to the American military industry, which the American Government was therefore serving to bolster, through in effect, a covert tax on the American people (Reuters). The Mubarak regime was kept in power by this American funding, given so that he would undertake to keep Islamic groups, in particular, the *Ikhwan* or Muslim Brotherhood out of power. Accordingly, Mubarak's loyalties were seen to lie more with the Americans and the Israelis than with the Egyptian people whose needs Mubarak tried, as argued, to ignore.[3] Mitchell's economic analysis of Egypt reveals how family-owned enterprise networks, with contracts to supply goods and services

---

3. This was a perspective communicated to me by Egyptian writers, especially Sahar El Mougy and Khaled Al Khamissi.

to the Egyptian military, also: "enjoyed monopolies [...] as exclusive agents for the goods and services of Western-based transnationals" (p. 13). He adds: "Nothing one reads in the documents of the International Monetary Fund (IMF) or United States Agency for International Development mentions the nature, history or power of these groups, whose existence was hidden behind the bland formulations of 'the private sector' and a revitalized 'Egyptian economy'" (pp. 13-14).

What might be said about the concept of a big society in this context? First of all, it concerns the "free-for-all" floating world of the global elites cut free from responsibilities to nation states, that is to say, divorced from local responsibilities while using local military and security services to protect its privileges as regards international alliances. Secondly, it concerns the "free-for-all" of policy-free, or welfare-free, de-regulated local societies. Thirdly, it also pertains to the success of political Islam. The popularity of political Islam in Egypt, that of the Brotherhood and of the Salafis, has been due to how these groups did take up the volunteering challenge of providing the services that the state was failing to provide. It was they who were providing charitable assistance and various forms of grassroots organization (Abdelrahman, p. 75). The result is that the Islamic groups attracted support while also serving to set up a mini-state of their own. Karim El Shenawy's new film *Salafi* (2012) provides a fascinating insight into what may be called "the Salafi big society". That is to say, in some ways, Islamic groups were inversely replicating the mini-states or colonies of the gated community world, but with global Islam rather than global capital as the over-arching system to be maintained.

What the Egyptian revolution means in the light of the above is surely over-determined. However, the kind of analysis offered by most Western commentators is drastically simplifying and misleading when the revolution is summed up in terms of the desire to overthrow dictatorship and political Islam in favour of a liberal, secular society, implicitly on Western lines, as argued by Žižek (2011).

In the light of Bradley's analysis, together with the novels of Al Aswany and Towfik, a different picture presents itself. That is, the revolution should be seen as primarily a revolt against neoliberal or gated community capitalism (in its impetus whatever its fate), more than as a desire to be (impossibly) assimilated into that "first world". This question will be returned to further on, to be more fully explicated in terms of "dignity".

Writing online in February 2011 to address the capitalist context of the revolution, Adam Hanieh notes at this early stage that: "the claim that this is a struggle for "democracy" acts to obfuscate more than clarify what these uprisings are about". The further point to be made here is that understandings of the Egyptian revolution differ according to whether it is viewed through pre-given Western templates (often tacitly informed by neoliberalism) or viewed through Egyptian popular and literary culture. One significant exception to the dominant portrayals of the revolution in a global context, those that assume capitalist democratic models, can be found in Walter Armbrust's article for *Al Jazeera* entitled: "A Revolution Against Neoliberalism?" Also written as the revolution was unfolding, Amburst is quickly alert to its implications, as spelt out in his title. I would conjecture that this may be in part because his intellectual perspective is informed by his close knowledge of modern Arab popular culture (Armbrust 1996) — having found such cultural sources to be especially pertinent in my own research — while Amburst's work also engages with the new School of Cairo Urban Studies, launched to study the material effects of globalization on Cairo and Cairenes with a volume entitled *Cairo Cosmopolitan: Politics, Culture and Urban Space in the New Globalized Middle East* (Singerman & Amar 2009; see also Salama 2007).

Of course, *Utopia* is a fantasy, both as a work of fiction and, in this configuration, as a notion, a matter of the brilliance of Towfik's novel. That is, what the novel implies is that its elite/outcast structure is in effect a fantasy, where certain commentators use the term "neoliberal utopianism" (Harvey, p. 37). A visual version of the semiotics of neoliberal utopianism can be viewed on You Tube, where advertisements for new greater Cairo property developments are posted. What these video clips show up is the extent to which the gated community form is a fictional world made concrete, one voice-over spelling out the fantasy appeal of its visual messages in stating, "Emaar Egypt invites you to share its dreams" ("Mividia New Cairo City Villas"). But further to this, the logic of this so-called utopianism is an anti-social one of a will-to-insularity, or self-sufficiency, therefore determining and casting any relation to others in the form of what can only be a denied relationality; with the return of the negated other, necessarily emerging in the form of negative projections: as sub-human, as animal, as lost cause, as criminal, as terrorist or as rebel.

August Riots and the Shrunken Society

The question that I wish to raise in this section is: if Mubarak's dictatorship could be seen as a question of neoliberalism, is there a way in which neoliberalism might be understood to be authoritarian? This would, of course, be contrary to its self-image as a democratic promotion of the free market, but this contradiction is a question of what is understood by *freedom*: a question previously entertained by Polyani (1954) in relation to liberal capitalism. Mike Davis and Daniel Bertrand Monk in fact state: "Neoliberalism, as Pierre Bourdieu eloquently warned us, is actually an *authoritarian utopia* that is nothing less than 'a program of the methodical destruction of collectives', from trade unions and mill towns to families and small nations" (p. x). In order to advance this perception, Stuart Hall's analysis in *The Guardian* of the Coalition's intensification of "the long neoliberal revolution" will now be drawn on. Hall writes:

> Neoliberalism is grounded in the "free, possessive individual", with the state cast as tyrannical and oppressive. The welfare state, in particular, is the arch

enemy of freedom. The state must never govern society, dictate to free individuals how to dispose of their private property, regulate a free-market economy or interfere with the God-given right to make profits and amass personal wealth. State-led "social engineering" must never prevail over corporate and private interests. (2011)

The supposedly dictatorial state is therefore to be shrunk as much as possible in a conflation of individual possessiveness with market fundamentalism. Hall goes on to say that the welfare state, from the neoliberal perspective has been dismissed in the following terms: "Its do-gooding, utopian sentimentality enervated the nation's moral fibre, and eroded personal responsibility and the overriding duty of the poor to work". It is amusing to juxtapose this with the views of the gated community protagonist in *Utopia*, as follows:

> In some way, the poor deserve the circumstances they find themselves in. They are less clever than our fathers. They are weak-willed and lazy. They let themselves be robbed all this time without lifting a finger. That's why they have sunk lower than animals [...] That's why I can't stand any feelings of sympathy towards them. (p. 154)

Hall points out that the Conservative neoliberals lack policies. The lack of policies, as with the Mubarak regime, is a case of a refusal or inability to assume the responsibilities of a government in many respects. And, if a government does not govern, then what does it do? It rules, or it polices. In his dissection of politics in Egypt, Bradley observes: "The military regime has played its cards very shrewdly, ruling not governing" (p. 204). Bradley points out that this is a matter of minimal interference, where the main goal of ruling, as opposed to governing, is just self-survival.

Whereas actual dictatorship concerns rule by a tyrannical individual who acts as a law unto himself, with neoliberalism as a dictatorial phenomenon this is not personal as such but rather a matter of a de-personalised tyrannical individualism that acts a law unto itself. The Big Society becomes in effect the shrunken society: in the shrinking of governance, in the narrowly reductive understanding of freedom, and in the prioritizing of security concerns. Considering authoritarianism as an outcome of neoliberalism, Harvey writes: "Forms of surveillance and policing multiply [...] The coercive arm of the state is augmented to protect corporate interests and, if necessary, to repress dissent" (p. 77).

Although of course Britain is a democracy, its neoliberalism may seen as its anti-democratic self-contradiction, a symptom of which is the widespread frustration on the part of British citizens that governments do not institute the policies they were elected to institute. Moreover, what replaces the absence of engaged politics is "policy-as-jargon", a reliance on mere jargon being a characteristic of authoritarianism, as I have analysed elsewhere (Rooney 2005). In addition, in such a situation and contrary to expectations, bureaucracy does not decrease (a supposed result of deregulation), but rather is given over to obsessive business-based goal-setting and a regime of surveillance to keep performance on target, often superfluously when the business model is not in fact relevant to what is really necessary: as regards, for instance, public needs in areas such as health and education.

The London riots could be construed as partly a response to this predicament of neoliberal paralysis and partly a symptom of it. The two most striking features of the riots concern the ineffectuality and incompetence of the authorities; and the lawless, both chaotic and partly criminal, course of events. Gillian Slovo's play *The Riots*, consisting of an amalgam of view points across the community of the rioters and the public sector, offers ample evidence of this. Firstly, rioters, police and members of the general public all speak of the lack of the procedures available in confronting the riots, one man commenting: "I just saw police runnin' around like dickheads doin' nothin' innit like" (p. 33).

In that this cluelessness derives, at least in part, from a lack of effective policies with respect to urban underclasses in the first place, what the play *The Riots* enables us to grasp is that the government's policy towards this class seems to have mainly been one of treating its deprivations as primarily a policing problem characterized by two particular approaches. Here, as touched on at the outset of this chapter, one approach is the automatic and performative demonization of this class: a case of blaming the victims. (I use the term "performative" in the philosophical and linguistic sense which denotes a speech act that is meant to institute its own reality). Camila Batmanghelidj considers the workings of this mechanism of interpellation, as follows: "The minute you start describing the poor as the lazy you split off a large section of society by er humiliating them. The underclass was described as 'amoral'. And this is very important in terms of how people ended up behaving" (p. 43).

The other approach entailed in treating the underclass as but a policing problem is a question of supervising the movements of its members. "Stop and search" is an infamous example of such. Equally unpopular are dispersal zones. Sadie King states:

> The thing that I really object to is the way young people are treated in Hackney generally by ... the police ... They have very fast quick-fix policies that are quite brutal, um the main one being dispersal zones [...] It creates [in] kids of like 10 this kind of anti-state, you know, anti-police culture, and they see themselves as labeled and they see the police as there to interrupt them. (p. 44)

One message of the riots may be heard as: "all you ever do is police us, and we are sick of that; if you're going to leave us alone, leave us alone then".

While, as argued, the Egyptian revolution and the London riots may both have been triggered by similar flash points and questions of structural inequality leading to a point of intolerable humiliation and anger, the two events are yet quite different in their manifestations, or what may be termed "languages".

The Revolutionary Language of Dignity and the Riotous Language of Pride

Poet Lemm Sissay in a blog entitled "Who Are the Criminals?" considers the riots in terms of an English spring, and objects of a citizen journalist reporting the riots in a negative way: "There was no excited fervour in his voice like that of reporters on the riots of the Arab spring". However, it has to be said that the scenes of the Egyptian revolution were genuinely inspiring and uplifting, while the scenes of the English riots, seen in such a light, appeared embarrassing — where the challenge is to grasp this in a humourous manner, as will be argued. While Tahrir Square could be described as a festival of collective creativity, the language of the riots was largely one of consumerist looting and terrorizing arson. Why were there such dramatically different forms of expression? And why does Sissay seek to negate the difference between Midan Tahrir and the riots?

It is necessary to appreciate where Sissay's objection may be coming from. It seems to be over the question of performative labelling that this essay has aimed to address. That is, the rioters are *automatically* dismissed, merely continuing the automatic demonization of the underclass in the first place. Sissay objects to Cameron defining the riots as "criminality, pure and simple" and to Teresa May's similar tactic in speaking of "sheer criminality". As a neoliberal response, the blanket labelling is a typical evasion of responsibility at the same time that it is a typical resort to a pre-given form of categorical structuring. It could be called "lazy". What may be suggested is that the categorical construction of a criminal class is set up as a kind of dumping ground to deal with or evade the criminality of class, implying the disavowal: "we are not guilty of irresponsible insularity; it is those we isolate or cordon off as criminals who are". What is most telling is Cameron's "pure and simple" (implying "so I wash my hands of it"), as regards this performative gesture.

Sissay is correct to raise the question of: who, in fact, are the criminals? This was a question I revolved in a *Counterpunch* article as the riots broke out, (Rooney 2011) while in *The Riots*, MP John McDonnell states: "Society has created a society of looters at every level: MPs fiddling expenses, bankers with their bonuses, corporations not paying their taxes, and all this was, was kids with the same moral values that have been inculcated in society motivated by the same level of consumerism, um coming out and seizing their opportunity" (pp. 53-54). That said, such evident cynicism is more than a case of complicity in that the rioters were, in effect, staging a parody of the Big Society and its rhetoric, and, by such a means, exposing its pretensions. That is, while the message of the Big Society initiative is "help yourself", this is exactly what the rioter-looters did, interpreting the dictum just as the "fat cats" (as opposed to philanthropists) were widely perceived to. The behaviour of the rioters showed the ethical hypocrisy entailed in the discrepancy between "the goods" of free market "help yourself" economics and "the good" of social self-help. In addition, the "free-for-all" ethos of market fundamentalism was parodied and exposed. A "free-for-all" can refer to a fight with multiple fighters and no rules: the prettifying jargon of the Big Society masked what could otherwise be more concretely perceived as a de-regulated brawl in a society where things are not really free. It was actually quite funny, apart from the violence. As Mohamed Hammoudan (a man whose house was burnt down) states of witnessing the looting scramble: "I just had to start laughing" (*The Riots*, p. 28).

The riots were almost, but not quite, carnivalesque. In a carnival, the poor get to act and send up the roles of their oppressors (Bakhtin 1984). One rioter in an interview says: "They was the criminals today. We was enforcing the law" (Prasad 2011). The question to pose here is: yes, but seriously?

Could the rioters see the joke? The Egyptian revolution has been dubbed "the revolution of the joke": *al-Thawra al-daHika*. Salem and Taira maintain the joke may be said to entail an upsetting of expectations (Mehrez, p. 194). However, the language of the riots may be said to have actually reinforced the social expectation of "possessive individualism", in Hall's phrase, but more seriously than ever intended, placing the onus on neoliberal advocates to say: "that stuff about possessive individualism, we was only joking, innit".

The scenes of the riots tellingly evoke theories of colonial mimicry, especially those of Bhabha (1994). For Bhabha, the colonised through mimicry of the colonisers act as mirrors in which the colonisers (or here elite) are able to see themselves disturbingly or grotesquely reflected. However, for Bhabha, there is no alternative to the structure of colonial expectations, no outside. In such a framework, the mimetic behaviour of the rioters could be understood to have partially subverted yet ultimately maintained the structure of neoliberal expectations.

Lilia Labidi in an article on Egyptian humour prior to the revolution, which appeared in 2006, offers an alternative understanding towards grasping the humour of the revolution. Interestingly, Labidi provides the following context for her study of Nagui Kamel's cartoons: "The deregulation that liberalization imposes gives a predominant role to the strongest and transfers costs to the weakest" (p. 27). Kamel's cartoons depict disempowered Egyptian citizens caught in positions of embarrassment and humiliation struggling to maintain their pride. An example of such is a man in his underwear begging his boss for a loan with the byline: "In truth, the first loan did n't completely cover me" (p. 34). The humour may be said to depend on not judging these characters according to the social expectations by which they are forced to act. For Labidi, this is a matter of "sympathy not hatred", and a matter of abstraction, intellectualizing the predicaments shown: which I think is a case of not taking the humiliating situations personally. For Labidi, this effects a change in consciousness that she specifies as "self-transcendence". She also states: "The concentration of several cartoons around one subject allows, via humour, for a truth to emerge, a truth which up until then was masked" (p. 41). If we imagine a cartoon version of the riots, we would laugh sympathetically at the "me-tooism" mimicry (Slovo, p. 39) towards understanding the truth that is masked by the mimetic desire.

The fact that Sissay wishes that the citizen journalist he objects to might see the rioters in the same light as the revolutionaries indicates a sensitivity over the *image* of the rioters, and this directs us to a consideration of the riots as a matter of pride. In what follows, I would like to explicate the difference between the Egyptian revolution and the English riots in terms of a brief clarification of the difference between dignity and pride.

At the outset of this essay, a similar flash point for taking to the streets of Cairo and taking to the streets of Tottenham was identified in terms of certain lives being treated as if they had no value. In Egypt, this was something that came to be widely articulated in terms of dignity. In fact, Bradley in his book that predicts the uprising has a chapter entitled "Lost Dignity". Johnny West a journalist who, unlike Bradley, was totally surprised by the Arab Spring, wrote a book in which he describes trying to make up for his ignorance through talking to a wide cross-section of Egyptians about what their revolution is about. He speaks of finding *karama* (dignity) to have been the crucial motivation.

The initial protests in Tottenham could be considered a question of dignity, particularly as regards the callous treatment of Mark Duggan's family. However, the riots that ensued seem to be more about pride than dignity, in that looting does not confer dignity. In terms of neoliberal ethics, you are good if you are productive and your affluence acts as a sign of your moral worth, whereas if you are poor this means you are worthless. The consumerism of the riots, as a response to humiliation, indicates a certain internalization of the commercialization of human worth. As a form of self-esteem, pride, unlike dignity, has certain connotations of narcissism, self-display and self-importance as a reaction to inferiorization.

A closer analysis of the language of the riots is able to clarify some of the above. Regarding the looting, it could be a case of how commodity fetishism is used to counter depressed feelings of lack of self-worth. In Slovo's play once the rioters provide an insight into how this works in stating the following: "havin' a good pair of trainers around here is a way to bein' different calibre compared to everyone else" (p. 53).

This can be juxtaposed with Gautam Malkani's analysis of urban youth culture in *Londonstani*, where Malkani shows this culture to be obsessed with a "bling-bling" economy of aspirational affluence. For example, a character addresses his former teacher in text-speak as follows: "U cant chat to us about ambition n self-respect. U might got a bling fone but u drive a crapped-out 1980s Volvo n carry yo books round in a plastic bag innit" (p. 126). Although the Hounslow youth depicted in *Londonstani* are not poor, the worship of commodities is depicted in terms of self-esteem, and the need of the youth to "big" themselves up through lifestyle goods is, at bottom, not so much purely materialistic as symptomatic of lack of confidence (which is bound up with gender self-assertion too, see Malkani 2012).

The looting that took place in the riots may be related to some of the arson that took place in that psychological studies of arson indicate that those who engage in it often have low self-esteem (Dickens et al. 2012). While banks were understandably smashed and while some torching of shops appeared to have been intended in order to cover up evidence of looting, Slovo's *The Riots* indicates arson was also carried out for the sake of uplift, the expressions of the arsonists described in terms of "euphoria", (p. 26) as if the spectacular destruction conferred importance on them, for once; an "up-lifting" experience, so to speak.

In the Egyptian revolution, the early episodes of looting that took place were primarily orchestrated by the Mubarak regime releasing thugs (*baltajiya*) from prison to intimidate the demonstrators, while Tahrir Square protestors insisted on peaceful behaviour, Samia Mehrez stating: "There was no stampeding, no harassment, no violence, no strife" (p. 36). Mehrez, comparing the semiotics of Tahrir Square to those of the *mulids*, or Sufi festivals very prevalent in Egyptian society, writes:

> One of the most challenging aspects of the *mulid* is the management of enormous crowds that include families and small children. Human shields and human corridors are spontaneously created to protect participants and a sense of togetherness, camaraderie and closeness is the hallmark of a collective mood of merriment. All such rigorous organizational procedures became a daily affair in Mulid al-Tahrir as the sit-ins extended over time and the management of the political economy of the symbolic space of Tahrir became one of the most spectacular aspects of the revolution. These codes of communal solidarity and cohesion were crucial for sustaining and multiplying the crowds for they offered not just a sense of security in the midan but, more importantly, a new consciousness of what a *mulid* really meant within a revolutionary context. (p. 48)

The dignity of Tahrir is constantly associated with collective good will — self-respect through the respect of fellow citizens for each other, more than through a direct esteem of the self. What I wish to propose is that the pride/dignity dichotomy would seem to depend on the former being more a matter of individualism and the latter more a matter of a collective sensibility. The guilt/shame dichotomy has been widely understood in such terms, with guilt as individual and shame as collective (for a nuanced consideration of this, see Rose, pp. 1-14), but potentially comparable distinctions between pride and dignity have yet to be explored in contemporary discourse. In fact, the liberal philosophical tradition tends to posit dignity in terms of the recognition of individual worth, and often as an hierarchical affair: a question of stature and rank, beginning with the human as more elevated than the animal (see Riley 2010). While this cannot be adequately debated here, postcolonial approaches to the question of dignity place the emphasis on how those who humiliate others lose their dignity (Memmi 1965), where — as with Tahrir

Square — dignity emerges as a non-hierarchical and radically reciprocal form of social relationality.

Of course the riots were not homogeneous, and amongst their strands could indeed be found aspects of Tahrir festiveness and collective spirit. However, in comparison with the above depiction of the revolution by Mehrez, the riots might be understood as pre-revolutionary, closer to the dystopian, "colonial" world of Towfik's *Utopia* than to the real utopianism of Tahrir, which rendered the gated community class entirely irrelevant. In this, it put on view an alternative to a class-divided society, showing the world what a de-hierarchized and truly democratic society might look like. Tahrir turned the inward turning utopianism of the elites *inside out* effecting, I would argue, *a taking back of the power of the universal*: a re-affirmation of the people as constituting the value of the universal, and not capitalism.

What this opens up is the thought of a real big society or, let us just say, civil society.

Lost? or Civil Society?

Gillian Slovo's *The Riots* repeatedly stages the question of how different members of British society saw the rioters: they are asked to offer a description in just three words. The one term that comes up as reiterated across social and political divides is: "lost".

The term "lost" has different connotations. It can imply "loser" as opposed to "winner": those who are too hopeless to get ahead in life and who are to be left behind. It can also imply those who have lost their direction and therefore may need help to return to the way forward. Furthermore, it suggests those who have been lost sight of. This latter meaning is the most pertinent one for the considerations advanced in this article. The riots came as a surprise to many, indicating something that had been lost sight of. This in turn suggests that they pertain to the blind spots of society at large. While a blind spot may be spoken of simply in terms of lack of awareness, it is more than that condition of ignorant oversight in that it depends on what can be seen from a certain position, entailing unconscious projections.

Accordingly, what I wish to suggest is that if people were inclined to describe the rioters as "lost", then this indicates that they are unconsciously admitting to the possibility of their own worlds as having lost something. For example, when Gove calls the rioters "tragic lost souls", this could be heard as an involuntary admission that neoliberal Conservatism has lost its own soul. And if the rioters are repeatedly posited as lost, this should be seen as symptomatic of something that British society may have lost or stands to lose: most drastically, itself, its togetherness as a society, regarding everything that manifested itself in Tahrir Square in terms of mutual responsibility, care and dignity across divisions of class, gender and religion. While Tahrir Square showed us what a big society as public commons might look like, the August riots tended to make visible its absence in England.

In conclusion, while the Egyptian revolution is championed as a revolution for democracy by Western politicians and by the Western press, what has been much overlooked or deliberately ignored is that it was a revolution against neoliberalism. Mitchell, in his excellent essay (written in 2007, at a time we would now call "pre-revolutionary") to review the economic crisis in Egypt in the 1990s, writes: "The crisis of 1990/91 was not just a problem of public enterprises losing money or a profligate government overspending. It was also a problem of the so-called private sector and the chaos caused by deregulated international flows of speculative finance" (p. 7). He goes on to argue that the main impact of the IMF reform programme: "was to concentrate public funds into different and fewer hands The state turned resources away from agriculture and industry, and ignored the underlying problems of training and employment. It now subsidized financiers instead of factories, cement kilns instead of bakeries, speculators instead of schools [...] subsidized funds were channeled into the hands of a relatively small number of ever more powerful and prosperous financiers and entrepreneurs" (p. 13).

As a counterpart to this, the August riots, along with the more politicized Occupy movement, serve to raise the question of the authoritarian aspects of free-market neoliberalism. In addition, the implication is that the appeal for a big society is ultimately a revolutionary appeal. The point is well made by Jane Holgate and John Page writing of Hackney Unites community organization group:

> (F)or community organizing to work, it needs a target and an injustice that is deeply and widely felt. For communities like those in Hackney the widely felt and deeply felt injustice will be Cameron's attempts to redistribute wealth and power towards the already wealthy. The target will be Cameron's own policies. The only question is, when will he recognize that his Big Society will see the chickens coming home to roost? (Iskanian and Sretzer, p. 9)

This may be juxtaposed with Armbrust's conclusion to his article in *Al Jazeera*: "Egypt and Tunisia are the first nations to carry out successful revolutions against neoliberal regimes. [...] Egyptians might well say to America *uqbalak* (may you be the next)".

I have in this essay made use of a postcolonial framework of analysis. This is because, while the capitalism of colonialism is understood, a consideration of the transnational gated community world directs our attention to new configurations of the *colonial* logic of capitalism. Juxtaposing the Egyptian revolution and the August riots serves to leave us with the strange notion of neoliberal states effecting to colonize, through privatization and policing, their own countries, as if they are *their own* countries; Eric Denis speaking of Egyptian neoliberalism in terms of a "private democracy to come" (p. 50). While there has been public debate about whether the August riots were race riots as such, it may be observed that whereas colonialism impoverishes on racial lines, neoliberalism others poverty *as if the poor constituted a different race.*

Egypt, with less of a middle class than Britain, retains in its folk culture of the sacred and festive *mulids*, and popular culture more generally, a certain reorientation of values that in the space of Tahrir Square inverted elitist/colonial utopianism into the utopianism of a freely held common ground. As argued, the assertion of dignity concerns this common ground while the assertion of pride is more a question of image. Here, it is worth noting that what Newsweek dubbed "Muslim Rage" on its infamous cover of 24 September 2012 could be better understood as a question of Muslim pride in the context of riots, and therefore less divisively compared with other political expressions of pride.

Finally, when neoliberal elites appropriate for themselves a mere language of "anti-dictatorship", "freedom", "big society", "globalization" and so on, both the Egyptian and the British uprisings served to unmask the appropriative, fraudulent gesture for what it is, with the people attempting, in different ways, to get their cities back. Crucial to this endeavour is a decolonization of our language regarding the neoliberal appropriations of a vocabulary that does not fit with the economic: for it is irrational to colonize "freedom", to privatize "dignity"; to singularize and trade in "utopia".

References

Abaza, M. (2011) 'Cairo's Downtown Imagined: Dubaisation or Nostalgia?', *Urban Studies*, vol. 48, pp. 1075–1087.

Abdelrahman, M. (2004) 'Divine Consumption: Islamic Goods in Egypt', Cairo Papers in Social Science, Special Issue: Cultural Dynamics in Contemporary Egypt, vol. 27, no. 1/2.

Adorno, T. (2007) 'Letters to Walter Benjamin', *Aesthetics and Politics*, Verso, London. pp. 110–132.

Alaidy, A. (2003) *Being Abbas El Abd.*, Trans., Humphrey Davies, Arabia Books, London.

Al Aswany, A. (2004) *The Yacoubian Building*. Trans. Humphrey Davies, Fourth Estate, London.

Al Aswany, A. (2011) *On the State of Egypt: What Caused the Revolution*, Canongate, Edinburgh.

Albrow, M. (2012) "'Big Society as a Rhetorical Invention', The Big Society Debate: A New Agenda for Social Welfare", in Armine Ishkanian and Simon Szreter (eds.), Edward Elgar, Cheltenham.

Armbrust, W. (1996) *Mass Culture and Modernism in Egypt*, Cambridge University Press, Cambridge.

Armbrust, W. (2011) 'A Revolution Aganist Neoliberalism?', *Al Jazeera*, http://www.aljazeera.com/indepth/opinion/2011/02/201122414315249621.html (accessed 24 February).

Bakhtin, M. (1984) *Rabelais and His World*, Trans. Helene Iswolsky, Indiana University Press, Bloomington, IN.

Benjamin, W. (1969) *The Work of Art in the Mechanical Age of Reproduction*, Illuminations. Trans. Harry Zohn, Schocken Books, New York, NY, pp. 217–252.

Bhabha, H. K. (1994) *The Location of Culture*, Routledge, London.

Bradley, J. R. (2008) *Inside Egypt: The Land of the Pharaohs on the Brink of a Revolution*, Palgrave Macmillan, New York, NY.
Cameron, D. (2010) 'Our "Big Society" plan', http://www.conservatives.com/News/Speeches/2010/03/David_Cameron_Mending_Broken_Society.aspx
Chang, H.-J. (2011) *23 Things They Don't Tell You about Capitalism*, Penguin Books, London.
Davis, M. & Monk, B. (eds) (2007) *Evil Paradises: Dreamworlds of Neoliberalism*, The New Press, New York, NY.
Denis, E. (2009) 'Cairo as a Neoliberal Capital? From Walled City to Gated Community', *Cairo Cosmopolitan: Politics, Culture and Urban Space in the New Globalized Middle East*, American University Press, Cairo.
Dickens, G., Sugerman, P. & Gannon, T. (2012) *Firesetting and Mental Health*, RCPsych, London.
El Shenawy, K. (2012) Dir. *Salafi*, BBC Arabic, Egypt.
Fanon, F. (1961) *The Wretched of the Earth*, trans. C. Farrington, Penguin, Harmondsworth, 1990.
Hall, S. (2011) 'The March of the Neoliberals', *Guardian*, 12 Sep.
Hanieh, A. (2011) 'Egypt's Uprising: Not Just a Question of "Transition"', The Bullet, e-bulletin, No. 462.
Harvey, D. (2007) *A Brief History of Neoliberalism*, Oxford University Press, Oxford.
Labidi, Lilia (2004) 'Truth Claims in the Cartoon World of Nagui Kamal', Cairo Papers in Social Science, Special Issue: Cultural Dynamics in Contemporary Egypt, vol. 27, no. 1/2.
Malkani, Gautam (2007) *Londonstani*, Harper Perennial, London.
Malkani, G. (2012) 'Interview with Blake Brandes', *Wasafiri*, vol. 27, no. 72, pp. 17–18.
Mitchell, Timothy. (2007) 'Dreamland', in Mike Davis and Daniel Bertrand Monk (eds), *Evil Paradises: Dreamworlds of Neoliberalism*, The New Press, New York, NY.
'Mividia New Cairo City Villas', http://www.youtube.com/watch?v=BVPHsJbOD88&feature=reimfu
Mehrez, S. (ed.) (2012) *Translating Egypt's Revolution: The Language of Tahrir*, AUC Press, Cairo.
Memmi, A. (1965) *The Colonized and the Colonizer*, Beacon Press, Boston, MA.
Polyani, K. (1954) *The Great Transformation*, Beacon Press, Boston, MA.
Prasad, R. (2011) 'Reading the Riots', *Guardian*, http://www.guardian.co.uk/uk/2011/dec/05/riots-revenge-against-police
Reuters (2011) 'Factbox: Most U.S. Aid of Egypt Goes to Military'. http://www.reuters.com/article/2011/01/29/us-egypt-usa-aid-idUSTRE70S0IN2011129
Riley, S. (2010) 'Dignity as Absence of the Bestial: A Genealogy', *Journal of Cultural Research*, vol. 14, no. 2, pp. 143–159.
Rooney. C. (2005) 'On the Corruption of Language: The Poetry of Chenjerai Hove', in Robert Muponde and Ranka Primorac (eds), *Versions of Zimbabwean Literature: New Approaches to Literature and Culture*, Weaver Press, Harare.
Rooney, C. (2009) 'The Disappointed of the Earth', *Psychoanalysis and History*, vol. 11, no. 2, pp. 159–174.
Rooney, C. (2011a) 'From Cairo to Tottenham: Riots, Revolutions and Big Societies', *Counterpunch*, Weekend Edition 12-14 Aug., http://www.counterpunch.org
Rooney C. and El Desouky, A. (2011b) The Journal of Postcolonial Writing. Special issue: Egyptian Literary, Culture, vol. 47/4.
Rooney, C. (2013) 'The Contemporary Maqama in Egypt as a Form of Democracy' in Maggie Awadalla and Paul March-Russell (eds), *The Postcolonial Short Story: Contemporary Essays*, Palgrave, London.
Rose, J. (1993) *On Not Being Able to Sleep: Psychoanalysis and Modern World*, Princeton University Press, Princeton, NJ.

Sakr, R. (forthcoming) *Anticipating the Revolution: Literatures and Cultural Geographies of the Arab Uprisings*, Palgrave Pivot, London.
Salama, S. A. (2007) 'Gated Communities', *Al Ahram Weekly Online*, 9-15 Aug., http://www.ahram.org.eg/2007/857/op4.htm
Singerman, D. & Amar, P. (2009) *Cairo Cosmopolitan: Politics, Culture and Urban Space in the New Globalized Middle East*, American University Press, Cairo.
Sissay, L. (2011) 'Who Are the Criminals? (Part 2)', http://bloglemnsissay.com (accessed 9 August).
Slovo, G. (2011) *The Riots: From Spoken Evidence*, Oberon Books, London.
Towfik, A. K. (2011) *Utopia*. Trans. Chip Rossetti, Bloomsbury Qatar, Doha.
West, J. (2011) *Karama! Journeys through the Arab Spring*, Heron Books, London.
Žižek, S. (2011) 'Why Fear the Arab Revolutionary Spirit?' www.guardian.co.uk/commentisfree/2011/feb/01/egypt-tunisia-revolt

Critical Consumers Run Riot in Manchester

Sivamohan Valluvan, Nisha Kapoor and Virinder S. Kalra

This article attempts to unpack the manner in which the "shopping riots" narrative — a narrative of consumerism gone awry which became increasingly prominent in the popular characterisation of the 2011 riots — was operationalized. In doing so, we look to uncover the political saliences of the riots which this discursive terrain conceals. Whilst it is unsurprising that the violence which the riots staged met ritual denunciation, the historical significance of this rebuke lies in its discrediting of the riots as putatively lacking in any protest motive or grievance. The considerable stress laid on the imagery of looting alongside explanatory motifs of nihilism, vulgar materialism and gratuitous criminality all foregrounded a hubristic consumerist drive absent of an intelligible political subjectivity. Through specific reference to the riots as they transpired in Manchester, four related points of discussion will be adopted in critically assessing this portrayal of the riots as apolitical consumerism. We ask: (a) how does this framing result in the eliding of institutional and structural circumstances (e.g. police relations and labour market factors); (b) to what extent does such a characterisation of crass materialism borrows from already established racialised mappings of urban pathology; (c) what is the ideological status of the policy response which this characterisation licences; (d) and finally, how might we consider the political legitimacy of the riots from within the interpretative terrain of consumerism itself.

"Nothing will come of nothing. Speak again". (*King Lear*: I.1.90)

Introduction

In the wake of Mark Duggan's death, the unrest that engulfed England's capital from the 6th of August 2011 spread northwards, absorbing the cities of Birmingham, Liverpool and Manchester. In doing so, it constituted Britain's largest bout of disorder in recent history. By the time the riots had reached Manchester on August 9th, an influential national narrative had already begun to settle, spurred by Cameron's announcement outside Downing Street earlier that day that the ongoing disorder was "criminality pure and simple". Further affirmed in his speech to Parliament as the unrest drew to a close, the events were summed up as the "moral collapse" of a "broken society" perpetrated by criminals "with a twisted moral code, people with a complete absence of self-restraint". Declaring an "all out war on gangs and gang culture" to fight the "criminal disease that has infected [the] streets", Cameron's predictable solution was to call for enhanced securitisation and greater police powers. A flurry of headlines denouncing the "rule of the mob" (*Telegraph* 2011) and "anarchy" (*Daily Mail* 2011, *Sun* 2011) alongside complementary images of burning property and violent looting helped further this story. But as the narrative progressed, it was particularly this theme of looting which garnered the most attention, with emphasis placed on an excess acquisitive urge coupled to an unearned sense of entitlement, such that the term "rioters" began to be used interchangeably with "looters". This entangling consequently rendered the issue of *consumerism*, popularly termed as "shopping riots" (Williams 2011), its pivotal focus.

The imagery and commentary that emerged in the wake of Manchester's entry onto the rioting stage became central to the servicing of this alternative, yet increasingly efficacious mapping of urban dysfunction — namely, the riots as consumerist nihilism bereft of a "unifying" (Wilson 2011) political purpose. Central to our speculation here is that in Manchester it was very much the *city centre* which staged the rioting. The subsequent visual profile obtained by Manchester city centre and its recognisable branded façades — concomitant to its low-intensity violence and the impression of a relatively muted anti-police or anti-authority programme — accentuated the motifs of materialist consumerism. Another key feature in generating this interpretative line was the multi-racial composition of the riotous classes. The indelible impression that the participants in Manchester were "overwhelmingly white" (LSE and *Guardian* 2011, p. 14) ably put on hold certain intuitive attempts to "integrate the taken-for-granted racialised discourses into broader social and political explanations of the riots" (Solomos 2011, p. 3.1). And though Cameron had already signalled a move to lift the popular analysis beyond race, or anything else for that matter ("these riots were not about race ... these riots were not about Government cuts ... these riots were not about poverty"), the inadequacy of overtly race-configured discourses was intensified by the arrival of Manchester.

Consequently, through reference to details specific to Manchester, we wish to consider the ideological work undertaken when such bouts of urban violence are cast as *consumer riots*: a framing of disorder which locates the urge to loot at its centre. Newburn (2012) writes, in an intriguing article which speculates as to what Scarman would have made of the 2011 riots, that "the scale of the looting and the fact that, in some areas, the disorder had much more to do with mass opportunism than any grievance with the authorities would have looked quite different". Pictured as such, looting is no longer read as a common symptom of any broader sweep of violent unrest but as constituting the very drive of unrest. This spurious view attracted support from unexpected quarters such as the ubiquitous Žižek (2011) who phrased it, in an article titled "Shoplifters of the world unite", the riots represented "a violent action demanding nothing". A cluster of ascriptions congregate when the telling of the riots reductively foregrounds this putatively consumerist spirit: opportunistic, materialist, entitlement culture, "amoral" (Parsons 2011), "post-ideological" (Žižek 2011), "post-political" (Goodhart 2011a), and "an explosion of nihilism and hedonism" (Lammy 2011, p. 17). The discursive move here concerns in short a ready-at-hand ability to write out any manifest protest voice. Put bluntly, no politics, just looting. This dichotomy, we suggest, hinges on a disturbing refusal to even acknowledge a *premise* for discontent. "The most worrying thing about the [rioters] was their unpredictability and unashamed greed. There was no clear political agenda like London's recent G20 protests, and no common motivation like the racial hatred that drove the Los Angeles riots of 1992" (Wilson 2011). Though it was unsurprising that any sign of violence would automatically instantiate ritualistic denunciation, what is most intriguing about the subsequent dismissal is precisely this claim that it lacked a protest motive. Whereas rioting is traditionally discredited by caricaturing the protest cause from which it sprung, a more seductive discursive manoeuvre is to mute the political angle altogether.

We thus intend to unpack the manner in which the consumer riot narrative is operationalised and in the process uncover the political saliences of the riots which this discursive terrain conceals. We do so through adopting four related points of discussion: (a) how does this framing result in the eliding of institutional and structural circumstances (e.g. police relations and labour market factors); (b) to what extent does such a characterisation of vulgar materialism borrows from already established racialised mappings of urban pathology; (c) what is the ideological status of the policy response which this characterisation licences; (d) and finally, how might we consider the political legitimacy of the riots from *within* the interpretative terrain of consumerism itself. Whilst the first three themes address the ideologically expedient erasures of those political subjectivities which reside *outside* of the consumer drive, the final theme draws out, via a reading of Bauman, a political subjectivity to the riots from *within* the framework of consumerism.

The Flattening of Context

In expanding on a question posed by Murji and Neal (2011, p. 2.3), it is presupposed that the prospective settling of any "straightforward causal story" in the wake of rioting is to be read as ideologically symptomatic, as revealing of the broader ideological production of popular consent. In turn, the extent to which the frustrations which fuel a period of unrest are discredited needs to be situated in the commensurate extent to which the riots are captioned as *one coherent* event driven principally by consumerist opportunism. It is hereby important to first consider the manner in which such an explanatory frame relies on a flattening of the contextual variation as particular to the different sites.

The sealants that congeal to cover the cracks in such consumer riot narratives can be usefully dissolved through a simple comparison of Manchester and Salford. Though part of the same contiguous urban sprawl, Salford does not benefit from the consumer capitalism that has enabled Manchester to (re)produce itself, on the back of post-industrial decline, as an economically vibrant, cultural centre — i.e. regeneration. In contrast, Salford remains one of the most disadvantaged urban areas in the country, whereby it ranks joint-14th in the English index of multiple deprivation (Department of Communities and Local Government 2011). Yet the consumer riots narrative for both areas remained consistent, if suitably differentiated. The by-line, "As looters in Manchester made off with plasma TVs and clothes from Liam Gallagher's boutique, in Salford they were taking tins of food from Lidl and second-hand TVs from Cash Converters" (Clifton & Allison 2011), neatly captures the overarching manner in which discourses of consumerism can both contain and manage class. Evidently even "looters" can be *classified* in terms of the goods they choose.

Importantly, the autopsy of the Salford case indicates that a substantive element of the events of August 9th was in fact a recognisable form of protest politics targeting the state, a mode of anti-state mobilisation which the consumer framing cannot descriptively accommodate. Even though the ultimate locus of the events was the Salford Precinct — a shopping centre which was looted — the initial large-scale engagement took place on a housing estate nearby. Notably, a group of "around 100 school age children" were confronted by 50 riot police (National Centre for Social Research [NatCen] 2011, p. 20). This was followed by the firebombing of the local housing allocation office, where firefighters were also attacked as they tackled the blaze. In a one-year reflection, this distinction between Salford and Manchester with regard to the variation in levels of anti-authority activity is drawn as a way of justifying the allegedly inadequate police response:

> In Salford it was different again, with those involved attacking police and fire crews and destroying local community facilities. We have to be realistic that, in any situation, if a group of individuals choose to stand their ground and *take on the police*, it will take us some time to get sufficient officers to deal with it. (Sir Peter Fahy, GMP chief constable, quoted in *Manchester Evening News* 2012; emphasis added)

In a similar vein, the Chief Executive of Salford City Council — in a move to both individualise and localise but alas only within the terms of criminality — makes the following distinction: "In Salford the focus was very much on violence rather than theft, the rioters were older and we believe a lot of them were from Organised Crime Groups" (Barbara Spicer, quoted in Bennett 2011). Yet, despite the formal recognition that the events in Manchester and Salford were different, they are dealt with as symptomatic of the same unitary problem. The flattening of such contextual complexity into a unified narrative foregrounding a common materialist drive is perhaps best articulated by the church via a local parish priest, witness to the evening looting, who held accountable the supposed erosion of moral values and an entitlement culture of "consumerism" as "a recreational right" (Matthews 2011).

That the police themselves served as a target for the rioters should ideally have *complicated* the picture of simple criminality which the consumer riot characterisation draws forth. After all, the police at best constitutes a hindrance to any criminal purpose. To entice the police into direct confrontation generates an unnecessary complication which even the least witted of the "criminal class" would do well to avoid. Herein, any purposeful encounter with the police as documented in Salford suggests a different collective end, an end which better alludes to a structurally embedded hostility as opposed to a series of impromptu criminal whims. Indeed, to engage the police is to engage that interface of the state which is the most visible and immediate to those constituencies alienated from other common fields of state activity (e.g. education and the labour market).

Moreover, as Harvey (2011) flags in his short post-riots piece, to declare such disturbances criminal is a statement, which beyond its rhetorical potency, remains analytically hollow. Prolonged and diffuse occurrences of unrest do not transpire in the vacuum that many in the public debate would have us believe. When these acts are condemned as the contemptible deeds of mere "feral" criminals, an obvious question arises: where does the human cease and the criminal begin? Or are criminals simply a timeless class for themselves, forever constituted as such? The flippancy of the above becomes farcical when the debate is foreclosed at this level of criminality, a move spearheaded by figures as stately as the Prime Minister ("criminality pure and simple"). Put differently, the unpleasant fact that Salford hosts certain wards where unemployment breaches the 50% mark (*Economist* 2010) should surely figure in any final consideration of why such extensive upheaval manifested.

To instead shoehorn the deliberate anti-police mobilisations — and the undeniable allure of such confrontations in sustaining the crowd momentum required for any form of rioting (Bagguley & Hussain 2008) — into a one-dimensional narrative of consumerist criminality is in turn best understood by its *ideological* economy. In the formulation of a common consumerist narrative, a discursive space is cleared for a policy response relieved of any redistributive and/or legislative function. In short, a policy response neoliberal in purpose; a purpose which further authorises the retreat of the state from those jurisdictions which do not directly concern issues of security and/or the containment of threat (Goldberg 2009). It is, however, helpful — prior to a more extended policy-sourced discussion on the neoliberal forms of governance which the characterisation of the riots as consumerist allows for —

to briefly unpack the relationship between representations of race and the popular picturing of the urban consumer riot. Doing so allows for a fuller grasp of how this picturing, by animating already settled signifying fields of fear and distrust, is made popularly intelligible. Just as the merging of Salford and Manchester creates an ideologically effective occlusion, the rioter as "looter without race" plays a similar sleight of hand.

The Resilience of Race

A supposed easing of race to the margins of the explanatory picture is itself remarkable when contrasted to the discursive handling and policy aftermath concerning other recent bouts of urban unrest. These incidents have generally invited a racialised assessment, one which either foregrounds the criminal pathology of the black inner-city (1980's), or, when an Asian/Muslim presence was central, as in 2001, draws upon well-embedded attributions of self-segregation, cultural incompatibility and excess communalism (Kundani 2007). The multi-ethnic character, however, of the 2011 riots, and the "social and spatial complexity of cultural difference" which the riots evinced, seemed to "militate against those older and totalizing race discourses" (Murji & Neal 2011, p. 2.9). For instance, any ethnically referenced scheme of civilisational incompatibility as employed during and after the 2001 Northwest riots was postponed this time round as the imagery which circulated was not sufficiently elastic to either write out the presence of white bodies or persuasively account for the relatively (with regard to the cities at which the riots ensued) low Asian profile (LSE and *Guardian* 2011, p. 13).

Indeed, it might be suggested that witnessed at certain discursive nodes was a marked inversion of the otherwise commonplace inscriptions of fear and vilification which conspicuous expressions of a Muslim identity evoke. A brief glance at the Birmingham rendition of the riots provides images of young Muslim men huddled outside around Tariq Jahan whilst chanting in the name of Allah. These images are striking in that they did not anticipate conflict but signalled comfort and assurance (*Guardian Online* 2011). This momentary distraction from the characterisation of Muslims and their "insular" (Lentin & Titley 2011, p. 185) communal attachments as the principal source of national disorder is suggestive of the broader shift which these riots seemed to represent. This episode, anecdotal as it might be, bore witness to a different symbolic regime (vis-à-vis the locating of threat and social crisis) being operationalisaed in the assessment of the riots — whereby demonstrations of minority communal identity (consider also the lauding of Turkish shopkeepers turned Hackney "vigilantes") manage to obtain a positive charge when the threat to the values which keep the nation stable are relocated to the nihilistic, crass consumerism which is said to underpin the criminal disposition of urban working-class youth.

The suggestion, however, of a discursive shift from race narratives to a more general language of apolitical materialism should not be seen in mutually exclusive terms. Solomos (2011) rightly advises that a more complex analysis of the current riots discourse would acknowledge that the very intelligibility of references to "criminality and gang culture", "Broken Britain" and the depravations of "consumer-society" (2011, p. 2.1) when blame is apportioned benefits from these references being already freighted with allusions to the pathology of "black" culture and its patronage of lifestyle amoralism. The traction of the consumer riots narrative and its crass criminality rests precisely on the "stickiness" (Ahmed 2004) of racialised meanings whenever and wherever social disorder and the fears it foster is scoped. It is thus instructive to briefly sketch some of the lingering affinities that these discursive cues of nihilist materialism and wanton criminality share with the already well-established representational standards concerning the degenerate *black* inner-city (or as Anderson (2012) phrases it, the "iconic [black] ghetto").

The most notorious instance of an attempt to resituate racialised meanings at the evaluative centre — whilst still conceding that the rioters were irreducibly diverse — was of course Starkey's startling claim during a *Newsnight* discussion that "the whites have become black". Whilst his comments received considerable attention, there was an impression amongst the left that Starkey represented an amusing outlier, quixotically trying to salvage the explanatory value of race (Merrick 2011). As welcome as that would be, it is evident that amongst a populist commentariat, there had already been multiple efforts to foreground the influence of black youth culture. Most notably in the *Telegraph*, which in the wake of the Tottenham riots itself, ran comment pieces by Young (2011) and Birbalsingh (2011) profiling the toxic influence of black gang culture. Such lines were picked up elsewhere too, most acerbically in Parsons' (2011) *Daily Mirror* column:

> Without the gang culture of black London, none of the riots would have happened — including the riots in other cities like Manchester and Birmingham where most of rioters were white. The snarling, amoral pack mentality of gangs that are too often a substitute for family, school and work made the riots possible. These youths were the shock troops of the riots, and its inspiration — even in the white riots of Piccadilly, Manchester.

In these moves, the consumer riot characterisation, whilst unable to couch the riots in the simplistic terms of multicultural crisis, does at various junctures seem to surreptitiously reinscribe racialised fears when making sense of Britain's riotous "underclass" and its materialist hysteria. A cultural theme of amoral opportunism central to the consumer riots narrative is funnelled into a broader "reflection" on the deleterious encroachment of an "imported Jamaican culture". This troubling picture was best elaborated in the essays penned by the influential Goodhart (2011a, 2011b). In formulating his typically unoriginal post-riots causal claim, Goodhart (2011a) held singularly responsible the "nihilistic grievance culture of the black inner city, fanned by parts of the hip-hop/rap scene and copied by many white people".

Clearly, even when a particular formation of the underclass is marked as multi-racial it does not prevent its pathologisation from obtaining a racial subtext. Paul Gilroy was particularly prescient in 2004 when he suggested that the anxiety resulting from the increased presence of minorities in the public sphere partly resided in the speculation that white life too might stand to be seduced by these "alien mentalities". In an accurate anticipation of the fears given expression to in Starkey's bumbling yet deeply troubling paleoconservatism, Gilroy (2004, p. 134) wrote,

> [I]nfluential pages of publications like *Prospect* and *The Salisbury Review* were groaning under the weight of speculations about the pathological characteristics of black culture, "black on black" violence, and, worse still, the transmission of antisocial alien mentalities into the urban dregs of wretched white, working-class life.

The heavy mileage of hip-hop in servicing such "transmission" alarms (most evident in Goodhart's pieces) should not be understated. It is precisely the presence of a public already literate in the representational cues of degenerate materialism tied to alarmist evocations of black hip-hop which renders instantly reasonable a general (across race) ascription to the rioters of a morally aimless cultural drive. Hip-hop, assigned a central role in the popular imagination as being the soundtrack of the urban "underclass" (or more properly put, the urban poor), is considered both the incubator and reflection of their dysfunction. In the final reckoning, it might be suggested that is only through these habitual racialised references (e.g. a black gang culture disseminated through the soundscapes of hip-hop nihilism) that the alleged *cultural* origins of the consumerist riot is made compellingly intelligible to the polity at large.

This instantiation of a racialised "culture talk" (Lentin & Titley 2011, p. 63) is of course particularly invidious as it refuses to even raise, despite trading extensively in the representational fields of race, the possibility of *racism's* continued relevance. This alternative way of talking about race which draws on racial images and narratives, whilst silencing race and denying racism, is symptomatic of what many have theorised as the post-racial present (Winant 2004, Goldberg 2009). In other words, a racial subtext is pressed without having to produce an accompanying racial text (i.e. the "looter without race"). The mode in which the media apparatus works for the state in this regard is signalled by *New Statesman* political editor Rafael Behr (quoted in Bassel 2012, p. 23) who noted that "there was something mildly ridiculous about a bunch of white men sitting in all-white newsrooms, asking white journalists on their staff if they knew any black people who might want to write about how racism is no longer such an issue". Embedding itself in such media climates, the characterisation of the riots as a violent and delinquent consumerism is particularly effective as it works to erase acknowledgements of racially structured inequalities from public conversation just as it uses racialised cultural maps to distinguish between good and bad consumers.

Policy and the Neoliberal Response

Having primed the manner in which the consumer riot is made intelligible to the popular gaze, it is now possible to locate the individualised culturalisation of social crises within the contours of a more general epochal drift towards neoliberal forms of governance. In other words, in persuasively generating an impression of the riots as apolitical in character, the state is in a position to formulate a decidedly apolitical political response (or in less oblique terms, a political response which further empties government of a redistributive, interventionist mandate).

As foreshadowed, reducing social unrest deeply rooted in structural conditions to cultural attributes is a well-rehearsed trope frequently brought out to absolve the state of any efficacious responsibility concerning popular unrest, and has featured prominently in responses to both the 1980s and 2001 riots. The response in 2001, in emphasising a heuristic of polar communities living "parallel lives" for understanding the violence, generated policies preoccupied with "community cohesion" to the neglect of strategies for addressing the entrenched material inequalities faced by the communities involved. The "community cohesion" package, which was able to foreground race whilst bracketing out both racism and economic conditions, spoke to a shift in policy orientation from the state and the majority populace to the disruptive cultural dispositions attributed to minorities, dispositions which the communities in question were to amend of their own accord. Whilst the state, at best, might facilitate "deep and meaningful interaction" (Commission for Racial Equality 2007, p. 25), it was the Muslim "communities" themselves who were to proactively exercise their duty to "integrate".

Though eschewing the vocabulary of community cohesion, the policy response set out in "After the Riots", the final report of the Riots Communities and Victims Panel (RCVP 2012, p. 5), was all the more prone to diluting the state's interventionist role. The report, primarily concerned with "how communities can be made more socially and economically resilient", set out six key areas in which this could be achieved. In stark contrast to the Scarman Report of 1981 or even the fraught Cantle Report of 2001, social and economic exclusion and the limited availability of education, employment and housing opportunities received scant mention. Instead, it was the individuals, the community, the voluntary sector and to a lesser degree business, that were to remedy any outstanding grievances.

As mentioned above, analysis at the national level — not least the generic mantra of "criminality pure and simple" — has not been without its localised critiques, and authorities in Manchester and Salford have been quick to raise the contrasts and specificities of the disturbances as they played out in their localities. Salford council leader, John Merry, cautioned that national research carried out collaboratively by *The Guardian* and LSE was to be treated with "considerable scepticism" in relation to Salford (Cordon 2012). But such a critique which seemed poised to lend itself to an analysis that articulates the spatial inequalities of wealth in Britain and the embedded structural exclusions which inform Salford's history, instead limited its objections to painfully modest, superficial concerns (e.g. not all people in Salford are hostile to outsiders). On the contrary, Manchester and Salford's policy approach has been to adopt (and slightly adapt) national policy themes. "The Tale of Two Cities" report by the Social Action and Research Foundation (2012) — which sets out recommendations for Manchester and Salford — does nothing more than transpositionally localise the national agenda. The five main policy areas acquiesce to national priorities by focusing on "a community-rooted model of family policy", "improving young people's resilience" and "their capabilities", and bettering "democratic accountability in policing", whilst Manchester City Council is to work with GM Business in the Community in encouraging businesses to address the causes of rioting as part of their corporate social responsibility.

The objections to casual ascriptions of criminality then did not extend to a more robust critique of the consumer riot characterisation itself, a reflection perhaps of the limitations to localism when pursued within the broader sway of neoliberalism's advance. Nor did the localised response trouble individualism as the appropriate register at which both the cause of and solution to the riots could be sounded. Under the rubric of the "consumer riot", young people were to be taught "personal resilience", "self-sufficiency" and "strength of character" (as identified in the RCVP report [2012, p. 49]) in order to improve their life chances. "Deferred gratification" which demonstrates "strength of character", was given particular prominence as a proxy marker differentiating the rioters from those who were deemed "successful" (RCVP 2012, pp. 49–50). Even business is gently asked to encourage through its branding schemes a more responsible consumer spirit (advertising which inculcates such virtues of deferral), though it is predictably unclear as to how this end is to be executed and how any such extra-entrepreneurial role is to be harmonised with their profit motive. All the while the cuts to Youth Services, the increased inaccessibility of higher education and the lack of employment opportunities which had been protested by young people as recently as 10 months before were side lined, indeed silenced. Instead, in a signature neoliberal move — wherein failure and success and its many vagaries are interpreted solely as the outcome of individual will (or lack of) — employment and better education would be hereafter attained only by those who are adequately determined.

This policy premium on assignations of individualised character deficiencies is further apparent in the approaches suggested for dealing with socially excluded families in general. Realising that those identified under the Government's already demarcated "troubled families" programme were not coterminous with "rioter families", policy intervention was extended, in a moment of semantic extravagance, to "forgotten families" — those also on the margins of society but not sufficiently so to be included in the poorest 120,000. Though the programme specifies early intervention, this intervention is not envisaged in terms of service provisions or material benefits. Instead, it merely emboldens a disciplinary agenda of monitoring the "problem families" and further delegates, in the context of cuts to public spending, a set of ill-defined, notional roles to communities as well as the voluntary sector.

The folding of this pre-existing programme into the general remit of a post-riots policy response neatly crystallises another important hallmark of the neoliberal state's modus operandi: the spectacle of discipline and containment. Lentin and Titley (2011) argue — when detailing the broader features of "neoliberal governance" — that in authorising the state's weakened role concerning the delivery of social justice, a particular ideal of "autonomous" subjectivity takes precedence: as a self-constituted and sole author of his/her own life. (Simply put, the individualism discussed above) Conversely, however, the very effectiveness of this self-image precipitates an *intensification* in the punitive, "managerial" (p. 169) role the state assumes vis-à-vis those constituencies who are commonly represented as "irresponsible" (p. 164) and "dependent" (p. 190). In short, the state's mandate, whilst certainly diluted on certain fronts, is reasserted at the level of surveillance and containment (Kapoor 2011). The consumer riot characterisation, with its accented stress on individual dysfunction, ably feeds this dual securitising function. A more concerted effort is made to *monitor* (as in the forgotten families programme) whilst the harsher magistrate sentencing guidelines and bolstered powers of daily policing (e.g. stop-and-search and stop-and-account) serve to make more conspicuous (though not necessarily efficient) the mechanisms of containment vis-à-vis those least disposed to observe the proprieties of a civic consumer etiquette.

In this regard, noting that the contextual trigger of "austerity" to the 2011 riots resembled in many ways the similar circumstances which prompted past moments of urban unrest, the manner of the state's *response* to the troubles pointed to a formidable progression of neoliberal rationales. The same ideological tools employed by the ruling Coalition to justify the fiscal politics of "austerity" were unfurled in the state's response to the riots. The key character premised themes of "building personal resilience", "hopes and dreams" and incorporating business through "riots and the brands" — whilst concomitantly entrenching the state's disciplinary function — offered unmistakably neoliberal frames for reviewing the disorder. The historical analogue for such a policy response is perhaps best captured by Bloom. Bloom notes that the report's panacean emphasis on the values of "personal character" is disturbingly redolent of the "Boy Scouts and an Edwardian ethos that was once the province of the public school" (2012, p. 104). Put differently, in scaling back the not insignificant protective gains of the post-war welfare state, the neoliberal rhetoric manifest in the report appears a palimpsest of early 20th century rationales during when the welfare state and a purposeful redistributive ambition was of course only at its most embryonic stage.

Consumer Citizens and Modern Protest

It is also analytically worthwhile to lift forth a political subjectivity to the rioters from *within* the lens of consumerism. Supposing that it is indeed so that much of the rioting in Manchester was devoted to the pillaging of certain high-street stores — not as an anti-authority expression but as one of materialist *desire* — this alleged psychic state of the rioters need not be propositionally read as an indication of the riots lacking a protest objective. It is equally valid to read the rioters as advancing — in a futile, oblique and desperate manner — a demand for greater access to a critical realm of self-expression which is otherwise denied to them. Namely, they draw bellicose attention to their frustrations as inadequate citizens, as inadequate *consumer* citizens. The spirit of such a claim is of course firmly situated within the arguments of Bauman, who is perhaps the most canonical voice in tracing the centrality of consumerist routines — of interaction with goods and markets — in the facilitating of sutured identity performances as well as undergirding demonstrations of self-worth and generating momentary impressions of certainty.

Given Bauman's import within contemporary sociology as well as his fondness for topicality, his initial post-riot comments in "Consumerism Coming Home to Roost" (2011a) received considerable attention during the many academic round circles held in the immediate wake of the riots:

> This was not a rebellion or an uprising of famished and impoverished people or an oppressed ethnic of religious minority — but a mutiny of defective and disqualified consumers, people offended and humiliated by the display of riches to which they had been denied access.

His reading can appear at first glance, despite the sympathy with which it receives the rioters, to chime discomfortingly well with the generic consumer riots script and the political illegitimacy the hegemonic centre ascribes to such motivations. Yet, whilst we have suggested that reducing the riots to consumerism is limiting and offers a convenient absolution of the state, it remains the case that there is something novel about the consumer economy which does render the protest form in contemporary English cities historically unique. We thus look to isolate here a few select points regarding our particular handling of Bauman's relevance in affirming the political significance of rioting, even when interpretively left at the level of consumerist opportunism. His most recent work, *Collateral Damage* (2011b), is particularly apt as it marks a more considered response to the current constitution of the consumerist citizen subject.

First and foremost, consumerism is not the same as consumption. To consume is a general feature of social existence across time and space. To consume signs, objects and pleasures for instance. Consumerism on the other hand pertains specifically to a type of relationship between the individual and the marketplace: the ability to navigate the market whereby superfluous material goods as well as transient experiences are obtained at a high frequency in exchange for capital (Bauman 2005, 2007). Herein, the consumerist ethos which Bauman sketches should not be confused, as is often the case, with mere gratuitous self-indulgence (i.e. excess *consumption*). Instead, his argument alludes specifically to the necessary attempts by which individuals "in a world shorn of traditional bonds of identity and social connectivity" turn to the market of ephemeral goods and experiences in hoping to "fill the void" (Gofton 2011). The relevance of this distinction is best apparent vis-à-vis the reconfigured maps of *inequality*. Premised as it is on purchasing power, access to such consumer driven repertoires of identity assertion is markedly unequal. The exercise of consumer choice — through which the "construction and maintenance of self-identity" (Davis 2008, p. 73) is channelled — intersects with divisions in income and other liquid assets. Consequently, material inequality does not only hinder equal opportunity to "offices and positions", to evoke a Rawlsian parlance, but increasingly structures the very abilities of individuals to communicate to their relevant peers an intelligible social identity and observe the status values relevant to their respective and multiple identities. Herein, a riot which is consumerist in spirit, draws attention to a debilitating exclusion from the realm of consumer choices; choices which when properly rendered with informed understanding of a social group's expectations and status field are likely to carry for those competent (both materially and culturally) individuals many social rewards. We also note that another definition of consumption is to burn up, to use to the limit, to exhaust, all of which provide suitable metaphors with which riots become something other than apolitical acts of looting.

Second, in further foregrounding Bauman's emphasis on social inequality — as opposed to his general treatise on the diffuse condition of uncertainty and unfreedom — it is also worth remarking on the relationship between consumerism and morality. In the chapter of *Collateral Damage* which most directly considers the question of consumerism, Bauman widens his casting of the consumerist net (2011b, pp. 72—82). Whilst already serving as the pre-eminent conduit for assertions of identity, it also "mediates" (p. 75), primarily through repeated small acts of gift buying (p. 76), the attempts by which individuals rescue their otherwise attenuated remit for care and concern for those around them. In its function as a "morality substitute" (p. 75), the consumer market "offers material tokens of concern, sympathy, well-wishing, friendship and love" (p. 75). "Shopping thereby becomes a sort of moral act (and vice versa: moral acts lead by way of the shops)" (p. 77).

In an argument which echoes Sayer's later work (2005), Bauman ably relates in this chapter the figuring of class inequalities in the contemporary capacity to act morally. In "attaching price tags to acts of goodness" (2011b, p. 75) such possibilities of care become "dependent on access to consumer goods"

(p. 79). Hereby, granting that consumerism does indeed take on this added function — wherein alongside affirmations of self it also obtains a moral texture — it is possible to further draw out the political spirit contained in any putatively consumer driven riot. Put differently, the rioters, in their demonstrative "materialist" violence, can be read as appealing to a frustration at being denied the basis by which contemporary citizens are expected to execute their most elemental human faculties (i.e. moral responsibility).

Finally, it is also instructive to note that consumerism does not simply involve a relationship between individuals and commodified *objects*. The term appeals in equal measure to *experiences*. Though the specific character of experiences is not extensively discussed by Bauman, it is clear that he is attentive to its importance: for instance, when he passingly employs the phrase "experience economy" to designate the prominence of commodified services which draw upon the "totality of resources of people's personality, warts and all" (2011b, p. 46). Indeed, the well-documented shift to a service-sector economy which favours "subjectivity, playfulness and performativity" (p. 168) partially bears witness to experiences being privileged as the more bankable commodity of capitalist cities.

Importantly, with specific regard to contemporary measures of exclusion, consumer experiences generate not only affective qualities but also spatial coordinates. The late modern city is engaged as a temporal routine threading together a series of consumer experiences — be it a visit to the cinema multiplex, a meal or a rendezvous at a franchised café or two. The distinctive feature being that the experience is contingent on an ability to buy, and buy discerningly. As Mbembe comments in a paper which details the recent formation of select urban environments within Johannesburg as appropriate to desiring "consumer publics" (2004, p. 374):

> Melrose Arch is sold to residents and visitors not as a theater of consumption but as a social environment, a "community," and a place where people come together to eat, dance, listen to music, enjoy a good conversation, drink coffee, interact, and be entertained (p. 394).

This hinging of a city's privatised core to the denizen's consumer capabilities generates a spatially charted exclusion; whereby the city's consumer hubs, within which affirming "social environments" emerge, are rendered inaccessible to those lacking in such capabilities. Kunzru (2012, p. 90), the author and essayist, comments concerning the relationship between experience, consumerism and exclusion which he glimpses in the Olympics-driven attempt at a regeneration of what planners wish to term "Stratford city": "Instead of citizens, we are now to be customers, and our right to the city is contingent on the agreement of the private owners of those spaces". Attention to these privatised formations of consumer-intensive social environments as sketched by Mbembe and Kunzru allows for a theorisation into how Manchester city centre post-regeneration engenders humiliating forms of spatial exclusion. Put bluntly, Manchester city centre, increasingly bereft of spaces which are not contingent upon purchasing power, transmutes into a fortified, yet impossibly alluring field of experience-cum-consumption.

The architecture critic Hatherley (2012) laments, during his recent excoriation of the humdrum city centres to be found in various "regenerated" English cities (Manchester being an emblematic case), that the inner domains of these renewed cities no longer hunger for a public good — whereby the city's *raison d'être* no longer rests in the cultivation of a shared and interactive agora. Instead, modelled on the influential gospel of regeneration, most popularly formulated by Richard Florida, Manchester's enviable profile as an attractive global city *Economist* (2010) rests on its appeal to, as well as presence of, an urbane class of self-styled creative innovators, entrepreneurs and students — the "Creative Class ideologists other favourite British city, Manchester" (Hatherley 2012, p. 149). In the prioritising of these subjects, cities like Manchester are gradually rendered "yuppiedromes", the frank yet efficient term coined by Hatherley. Given this context, the excluded poor not only experiences their inability to buy as generating penalties at the aforementioned level of self-affirmation, but find their very ability to access the city curtailed.

> The typical [...] streetscape of pound shops and groceries may be unaesthetic, but it represents interwoven circuits of production and consumption that are local and targeted at the people who are already here, instead of those developers would like to see coming, people with more disposable income and fewer social problems. [The] poorest will be shunted out. (Kunzru 2012, p. 87)

The profile of Manchester city centre and its glittering shopping facades during the rioting can be consequently seen as conveying a perfectly apposite form of political protest. Insofar as, it was the city centre from which these individuals are alienated that was put under siege by the rioters (in contradistinction to the riots as they transpired in London, the city was occupied from within). Yet, upon having gestured at these different social functions facilitated through the consumer act (self-affirmation, morality, and the urban experience) — and conversely, the costs borne by those who are unable to realise a consumer purpose — it appears as if the impoverished constituents that participated in the riots suffer from a double bind. They are condemned for engaging in acts of violence whilst being concomitantly condemned for having only a *consumerist* political grievance to support that very violence. The rioters, by virtue of their seeming refusal to contrive an already sanctioned, "valid" political grievance — in lieu of those consumer-oriented exclusionary forms that many of them experience on a more regular and intimate basis — find their protestations represented as silence.

This received impression of the riots as demonstrably failing to gesture at any broader collective ambition ("no common motivation" [Wilson 2011]) must be contextually understood within the prevalent discursive scripts which render certain forms of political action intelligible and others less so. With this in mind, the premising of consumerist desires as *apolitical* in character signals a telling discursive trap regarding the contemporary relationship between registers of felt exclusion (the consumer register) and the vocabularies available for articulating that felt exclusion. Through reference to Bauman, this final section of the paper has intimated that — though there is never a situation in the UK where both race and state institutions do not figure in the provocation and/or evaluation of large-scale public disorder — outbursts by those most economically deprived will increasingly contain a significant consumerist purpose as well. When the citizen is cast first and foremost as a consumer, it is reasonable to suppose that political unrest will find expression within the parameters of that very consumer ethos. Put differently, the "privatizing" (Bauman 2011b, p. 16) of social life into a set of individualised consumer routines begets corresponding forms of political response.

Conclusion

In foregrounding the consumer-generated frustrations which contributed to the rioter's occupation of Manchester, we ask the simple question "Why does a consumerist end discredit the protest significance of the riots?" It is perhaps Lear's query of Cordelia — "Nothing will come of nothing. Speak again" — that best distils the condition of exclusion we wish to make apparent. The rioters have to, like Cordelia, "speak again" in more acceptable terms in order to remain productive within late capitalist economic models of assertion — assertion through the ability to buy. Here, it is not just their speech that is about nothing. Their very existence marks a nothingness within the consumer economy. They can neither buy nor loot.

It is our contention that the themes of disenfranchisement and exclusion have to be couched within and approached from an integrated theoretical understanding of consumerism and the socio-political formation of citizenry. This emphasis on the consumer riots which we have addressed from within should not, however, detract from the earlier themes advanced. Our purpose is not to suggest that the consumer riots characterisation is all encompassing. On the contrary, only by remarking on and remaking the consumer characterisation of the riots — which when at its default setting is pejorative and relies upon problematic racial discourses — do we enable a dialogue between it *and* the narratives of structural disenfranchisement, drawing attention to the forms in which the two are interrelated. A dialogue which we believe is integral to any constructive attempt to understand the muted voice which haunts the riots. Cordelia's silence at Lear's instruction to speak again unleashed, as many know, a war that tore the state apparatus apart. What do we do today, in what language do we speak? This is the question that we have sought to ask in these pages, querying in turn the discursive terrain characterising the "shopping riots".

References

Ahmed, S. (2004) *The Cultural Politics of Emotion*, Routledge, New York, NY.

Anderson, E. (2012) 'The Iconic Ghetto', *The Annals of the American Academy of Political and Social Science*, July (642), pp. 8–24.

Bagguley, P. & Hussain, Y. (2008) *Riotous Citizens: Ethnic Conflict in Multicultural Britain*, Ashgate, Aldershot.

Bassel, L. (2012) 'Media and the Riots: A Call for Action', Citizen Journalism Educational Trust and The-Latest.com, http://www.the-latest.com/files/documents/Riots%20and%20the%20Media%20Report.pdf

Bauman, Z. (2005) *Work, Consumerism and the New Poor*, Open University Press, Maidenhead.

Bauman, Z. (2007) 'Collateral Casualties of Consumerism', *Journal of Consumer Culture*, vol. 7, no. 1, pp. 25–56.

Bauman, Z. (2011a) 'Interview: Zygmunt Bauman on the UK Riots', *Social Europe Journal*, http://www.social-europe.eu/2011/08/interview-zygmunt-bauman-on-the-uk-riots/

Bauman, Z. (2011b) *Collateral Damage*, Polity Press, Cambridge.

Bennett, M. (2011) 'The Salford Riots: The Best and the Worst of our City', *Solace Summit Wordpress*, http://solacesummit.wordpress.com/2011/08/16/the-salford-riots/ (accessed 16 August).

Birbalsingh, K. (2011) 'These Riots were about Race. Why Ignore the Fact?', *The Telegraph*, http://blogs.telegraph.co.uk/news/katharinebirbalsingh/100099830/these-riots-were-about-race-why-ignore-the-fact/ (accessed 7 August).

Bloom, C. (2012) *Riot City*, Palgrave MacMillan, London.

Cantle, T. (2001) *Community Cohesion: A Report on the Independent Review*, Home Office, London.

Cordon, S. (2012) 'Salford Council Leader Slams Guardian's Research into August Riots', *Mancunian Matters*, http://mancunianmatters.co.uk/content/13032687-salford-council-leader-slams-guardians-research-august-riots (accessed 13 March).

Commission for Racial Equality (2007) 'Response to the Commission on Integration and Cohesion', http://www.cre.gov.uk.

Clifton, H. & Allison, E. (2011) 'Manchester and Salford: A Tale of Two Riots', *Guardian: Reading the Riots*, http://www.guardian.co.uk/uk/2011/dec/06/reading-the-riots-manchester-salford

Daily Mail, The (2011) 'The Anarchy Spreads', *Daily Mail*, 9 Aug., p. 1.

Daily Telegraph, The (2011) 'The Rule of the Mob', *Daily Telegraph*, 9 Aug., p. 1.

Davis, M. (2008) *Freedom and Consumerism: A Critique of Zygmunt Bauman's Sociology*, Ashgate, Aldershot.

Department of Communities and Local Government (2011) *The English Indices of Deprivation 2010*, DCLG, London.

Economist, The (2010) 'More, please', *Economist*, http://www.economist.com/node/15731470 (accessed 18 March).

Gofton, L. (2011) 'Collateral Damage: Social Inequalities in a Global Age', *Times Higher Education*, http://www.timeshighereducation.co.uk/story.asp?storyCode=416416&sectioncode=26 (accessed 9 June).

Gilroy, P. (2004) *Postcolonial Melancholia*, Columbia University Press, New York, NY.

Goodhart, D. (2011a) 'The Riots at the End of History', *Propsect Blogs*, http://www.prospectmagazine.co.uk/blog/the-riots-at-the-end-of-history/

Goodhart, D. (2011b) 'The Riots, the Rappers and the Anglo-Jamaican Tragedy', *Prospect*, http://www.prospectmagazine.co.uk/magazine/riots-goodhart/ (accessed August (185)).

Goldberg, D. T. (2009) *The Threat of Race: Reflections on Racial Neoliberalism*, Wiley-Blackwell, Oxford.
Guardian Online (2011) http://www.guardian.co.uk/uk/video/2011/aug/11/birmingham-vigil-died-riot-video?INTCMP=ILCNETTXT3486
Harvey, D. (2011) 'David Harvey on the English riots: Feral capitalism hits the streets', *Climate and Capitalism*, http://climateandcapitalism.com/2011/08/11/david-harvey-on-the-english-riots-feral-capitalism-hits-the-streets/ (accessed 11 August).
Hatherley, O. (2012) *A New Kind of Bleak*, Verso, London.
Lammy, D. (2011) *Out of the Ashes: Britain after the Riots*, Guardian Books, London.
Lentin, A. & Titley, G. (2011) *The Crises of Multiculturalism: Racism in a Neoliberal Age*, Zed Books, London.
LSE and *The Guardian* (2011), Reading the Riots Report, *The Guardian*, http://s3.documentcloud.org/documents/274239/reading-the-riots.pdf
Kapoor, N. (2011) 'The Advancement of Racial Neoliberalism in Britain', *Ethnic and Racial Studies*, doi:10.1080/01419870.2011.629002.
Kundani, A. (2007) *The End of Tolerance*, Pluto Press, London.
Kunzru, H. (2012) 'East End', *Intelligent Life*, July/Aug., pp. 82–90.
Manchester Evening News (2012) 'Greater Manchester Police Chief Sir Peter Fahy: No-one would have Backed us if we'd Cracked Down Hard on Rioters', *Manchester Evening News*, http://menmedia.co.uk/manchestereveningnews/news/s/1585350_greater-manchester-police-chief-sir-peter-fahy-no-one-would-have-backed-us-if-wed-cracked-down-hard-on-rioters (accessed 6 August).
Matthews, H. (2011) 'The Salford Riots and the Greed of the Disenfranchised', http://www.guardian.co.uk/commentisfree/2011/aug/10/salford-riots-greed-disenfranchised.
Mbembe, A. (2004) 'Aesthetics of Superfluity', *Public Culture*, vol. 16, no. 3, pp. 373–405.
Merrick, J. (2011) 'Starkey Raving Bonkers! Historian Accused of Racism on Riots', *The Independent*, http://www.independent.co.uk/news/uk/crime/starkey-raving-bonkers-historian-accused-of-racism-on-riots-2337441.html (accessed 14 August).
Murji, K. & Neal, S. (2011) 'Riot: Race and Politics in the 2011 Disorders', *Sociological Research Online*, vol. 16, no. 4, http://www.socresonline.org.uk/16/4/24.html.
National Centre for Social Research (2011) *The August Riots in England*, NatCen, London.
Newburn, T. (2012) '30 years after Brixton, what would Lord Scarman have made of the 2011 riots?', *Guardian: Reading the Riots*, http://www.guardian.co.uk/uk/2012/jul/01/brixton-lord-scarman-2011-riots
Parsons, T. (2011) 'UK Riots: Why did the Riots Happen? Who are the Rioters? What can we do to end this Madness?', *The Daily Mirror*, http://www.mirror.co.uk/news/uk-news/uk-riots-why-did-the-riots-happen-who-147237 (accessed 13 August).
Riots Communities and Victims Panel (2012) 'After the Riots Report. The Final Report of the Communities and Victims Panel', http://riotspanel.independent.gov.uk/wp-content/uploads/2012/03/Riots-Panel-Final-Report1.pdf
Sayer, A. (2005) *The Moral Significance of Class*, Cambridge University Press, Cambridge.
Scarman, L. (1981) *The Brixton Disorders 10–12 April 1981: Report of an Inquiry by the Rt. Hon. The Lord Scarman OBE*, HMSO, London.
Social Action and Research Foundation (2012) *The Tale of Two Cities: Complex Causes, Complex Solutions*, SARF, Salford.
Solomos, J. (2011) 'Race, Rumours and Riots: Past, Present and Future', *Sociological Research Online*, vol. 16, no. 4, p. 20.
Sun, The (2011) 'Anarchy', *Sun*, 9 Aug., p. 1.
Williams, Z. (2011) 'The UK Riots: The Psychology of Looting', *Guardian CiF*, http://www.guardian.co.uk/commentisfree/2011/aug/09/uk-riots-psychology-of-looting

Wilson, P. (2011) 'The Scariest Thing about the Rampaging Mob is the Lack of a Unifying Cause', *The Australian*, http://www.theaustralian.com.au/news/world/the-scariest-thing-about-the-rampaging-mob-is-the-lack-of-unifying-cause-peter-wilson-writes/story-e6frg6so-1226111544508

Winant, H. (2004) *The New Politics of Race: Globalism, Difference, Justice*, University of Minnesota Press, Minneapolis, MN.

Young, T. (2011) 'The Disturbances in Tottenham Tonight are Profoundly Depressing', *Telegraph Blogs*, http://blogs.telegraph.co.uk/news/tobyyoung/100099808/the-disturbances-in-tottenham-tonight-are-profoundly-depressing/

Žižek, S. (2011) 'Shoplifters of the World Unite', *London Review of Books*, http://www.lrb.co.uk/2011/08/19/slavoj-zizek/shoplifters-of-the-world-unite (accessed 19 August).

Regional Narratives and Post-racial Fantasies in the English Riots

Gargi Bhattacharyya

This article considers the manner in which the urban disturbances across England in 2011 were framed in popular and scholarly understanding. The article suggests that the days of rioting are not, in themselves, the events that merit analysis and scrutiny. Instead, we should consider again how we frame urban unrest within a broader analysis of the renegotiation of public space and national identities. The article goes on to consider the representation of regional characters in coverage of the riots and to present an analysis of fantasies of the post-racial that emerged in relation to events in Birmingham.

If you lived in Britain in the summer of 2012, you might have believed that the population was undergoing a thorough, successful and, most of all, highly enjoyable review and renewal of the meanings and practices of national identity.

The combined aftermath of the Queen's Jubilee and the London Olympics led to a widespread and often self-congratulatory discussion of the evolving and confident nature of British identity. For some years, previous to this apparently happy moment of conscious rebirth, British political life had returned repeatedly to the question of national identity, and in far from happy ways. From Tony Blair's evening lectures on the history of Britons and fabrication of the "respect" agenda to Brown's anxious defence of Britishness in the face of pretty open anti-Scottish prejudice to Cameron's retort of broken Britain as the alleged outcome of all of these years of New Labour nation-building, the lived culture of nationhood has been considered to be a political problem in recent years, something that needs fixing by the political class in one way or another.

Within this, Britishness has been a fraught term — something to tussle over, but also something uncomfortable, not quite right, always out of step with the more easy spaces of the popular where identities are lived with pleasure.

What changed in the summer of 2012 was a widespread popular will to remake and enjoy the shared spaces of national identity, most of all through an appeal to popular culture. I do not mean here to suggest that Britain has been immune from the kind of banal flag waving nationalism identified by Billig — quite the opposite, and these successfully popular celebrations engaged these mundane rituals of nationhood extensively — yet the genuine and surprising (including those taking part in the spectacle or feeling the unfamiliar feeling of patriotic pride, apparently, see Jeffries 2012) enthusiasm for belonging to a Britain that was self-deprecating and funny, party-friendly and culturally influential without being stuffy, bossy or overbearing and moved by the spirit of Freddy Mercury rather than Queen Victoria seems important to note. Something has been happening, however briefly.

Here, I want to reconsider the less-celebrated events of summer 2011 in the context of this will to reimagine the nation in hard times — and to suggest that even in these attempts to reframe Britain as a space of inclusion, old and new racisms play a part in defining the terms of belonging. A reworking and rewriting of the boundaries of popular nationhood remains a disciplinary process, even if it appears to be a loosening rather than a tightening.

Between the spring of 2011 and the summer of 2012, Britain engaged in a series of very public and highly staged enactments of shared identity, both official and impromptu and also, on occasion, a mixture of the two. In April 2011, considerable resources were dedicated to rehabilitating the royal family through the public celebrations of a royal wedding. This was heralded as the beginning of a long festive lead-in to the jubilee year and the public party of the London Olympics. For all the good-time talk, it was pretty clear that Britain was a place seeking to renegotiate the terms of public space, national identity and conviviality or even just practice a simple non-violent indifference that could lead to peaceful co-existence. Interspersed with these tightly choreographed public spectacles were the more freelance displays of urban unrest, Occupy camps and trade union demonstrations — yet these events also shared some themes with the public pageantry celebrating a kind of togetherness in the street as a version of shared identity through practice.

It is possible — although perhaps a little contrary — to consider the 2011 riots as one more episode in this longer renegotiation of public space, shared and divided identities, ownership and belonging. Perhaps the inclusion of "riot" as an aspect of negotiation appears perverse, but we should remember that negotiation takes many forms ranging from polite conversation to outright violence. If we deny the possibility that riot may represent an element in this wider renegotiation of public space and belonging, we seem to refuse the possibility that riot can be a form of meaningful action. To suggest that riotous behaviour is also a kind of response and intervention in this negotiation is not to argue that "riot" is, in fact if we could but see it, a political movement. I do not think that the English urban disturbances of 2011 represented an explicit project, despite some evidence of tactical co-operation by looters in some spaces. However, I do wish to present the negotiation of public space as a broad and messy endeavour that can encompass the unruly behaviours of riot as one response to uncertain and changing boundaries and shifting senses of allegiance and acceptability. In particular, I want to suggest that the events of August 2011 form only one part of a larger process of renegotiation in this particular period — one that encompasses both a coming to terms with post-imperial identities for some Britons and a reimagining of the relationship between citizen and state across austerity-struck Europe. In what follows, I consider one narrative strand in the coverage of the riots and suggest that, as always, the manner of this narrative tells us something about the consciousness of our times.

The Event of "Riots"

Some months on from the media hysteria surrounding the riots, it can be hard to remember what all the fuss was about. Although it is understandable that such brief but spectacular expressions of popular unease ignite public debate, perhaps one week in August is better understood as one moment in a period of wider uncertainty and contestation. There is no doubt that something happened — but perhaps what is significant can be discerned only by moving beyond a focus on those few days.

In the summer of 2011, the escalation of street unrest, looting and taking of public space in open defiance of the police and other authorities caused a corresponding frenzy of debate, speculation and anxiety. A little over a year after Cameron had become Prime Minister by forming a coalition government with the LibDems, after coining campaign slogans calling for a mending of broken Britain, it seemed that the Cameron analysis had been proved right. Here was the proof that Britain was, in fact, broken and that a significant section of society was eager to embrace the opportunity to smash things up, help themselves to desirable consumer goods, random sweeties and cans of pop, hang out in the street and defy the authority of the police. These happenings seemed to confirm Cameron's claim that this was a nation in need of some serious healing.

This piece begins from a position of doubt in relation to the significance of the riots. My doubt arises as a result of the following observations:

- Street violence is not unusual, and it could be argued that collective public disorder is embedded and tolerated in British popular culture.
- There have been numerous other instances of sustained public disorder across Europe and other parts of the world in recent years.
- The structure of feeling that riots are alleged to embody cannot be understood without a wider analysis of events — and this leads to an uncertainty about which moment is the "event".
- The 2011 riots are incomprehensible without reference to the longer history of riots and the interpretation of riots in Britain, because this is the symbolic arena shaping these actions.
- The continuities between the riots and other public reimaginings of national identity and relations between citizens seem more interesting than any attempt to identify the singularity of the riots as an event in themselves.

Most of all, the will to uncover the cultural meanings of the riots demands that these events and the accompanying narratives are placed in some context of sense-making in our time — inevitably, this process unsettles the idea that the riots in themselves constitute the significant event.

The Banality of Street Violence

It seems contrary to suggest that there was nothing unusual about the events of August 2011. The levels of disorder, numbers of people participating and geographical reach of the 2011 events far surpassed the urban unrest of recent decades. In addition, there quickly appeared to be a consciousness about these events that singled them out. Although many described the sensation of being caught up in the swell of the crowd and the excitement of the moment, the use of social media and the rapid transfer to other locations indicated a new awareness that a space of (temporary) disorder was opening. In part, this shared consciousness via social media was little more than a rhetorical thumbing of the nose to authority — as seemed to be the case with small-town calls to "riot" that went unheeded but, nevertheless, garnered punitive sentencing. Yet, the advent of social media means that we have some sense of how an explicit consciousness around participation in some major collective happening can be articulated and quickly shared among many. This alone marks out the events of 2011 and goes some way to explain the mechanics of the rapid and incremental spread of a temporarily shared consciousness or, at least, shared curiosity.

However, despite this aspect of newness, taking the riots as a standalone and uniquely significant event can seem to imply that street disorder is an unusual occurrence. Yet, the coding around the concept of "riot" excludes much of the street disorder so prevalent in Britain. The widespread disorder, violence and criminality that continues to characterise many town and city centres on Friday and Saturday evenings may be vilified and presented as a serious social problem, but it is not categorised as "riot", either legally or in popular imagination (Doyle 2010). Equally, the destruction wrought in the aftermath of many football matches in urban communities may result in arrests but not the framing of "riot". When considering the extent of the alleged contagion, it might be helpful to think again about what level of disorder is seen to constitute a riot and when and why such a demarcation is made.

Living in a Time of Disorder

Despite other instances of violent protest in the face of austerity measures among European neighbours, Britain retained a characteristically and resolutely national perspective when considering the events of August 2011. The various impacts of cutting welfare and pensions and, increasingly, the unbearable burden of austerity measures in terms of living conditions for ordinary people led to a series of events across Europe where taking the street became, once again, an important symbolic marker of popular voice.

From the mass protests against pension changes in France in 2010 (Fraser 2010), to the long-running unrest in response to the imposition of austerity measures in Greece (Maltezou & Papachristou 2011) to the indignados of Spain (Tremlett 2012), Europe has been undergoing a series of battles over the relationship between government and population and the ability to give voice to popular opinion, most clearly in relation to the varied and drastic changes in state provision undertaken in the name of austerity.

The majority of these other examples of urban unrest presented a conscious and explicit politics — some were formal and organised protests, the kind that you can put in your diary, and others were eruptions that occurred alongside such explicit campaigns, but nowhere in the British media was it suggested that this other unrest was an expression of animalistic nature or a collapse of social contracts.

I do not want to argue here that spontaneous street disorder and looting is the expression of some nascent emancipatory politics. However, much British commentary fell quickly into accounts that could imagine few options between criminality and organised political movements — the suggestion that some forms of (momentary mass) criminality which might be a symptom of some larger political formation was given little consideration in popular debate. Perhaps the disorder in Britain was quite different from the disorder in other parts of Europe, but perhaps also these cracks in public order in many places indicate something of significance about our moment. The question may be less about the brokenness of Britain and more about various popular responses to the questionable legitimacy of government in the face of global economic crisis.

Identifying the Beginning and the End

Street disturbances can give a mistaken sense of certainty to those seeking to define their object of study. We know when things started to get rough, how long all this lasted and when things, purportedly, returned to normal.

Yet, the various commentaries have all implied other starting points — almost no one argues that the killing of Duggan is the very beginning. This terrible incident may have been the immediate spark, but the orthodoxies of riot analysis remind us that the ostensible trigger is a reminder or reference to longer standing grievances or tensions. The point of interest, then, is not so much why this incident ignites this chain of reactions, but why so many other incidents do not. There has been no shortage of police killings in recent years — among them, Kingsley Burrell and Demetre Fraser in Birmingham, Anthony Grainger in Manchester and Smiley Culture in his own home, a death that caused a great deal of concern and protest in Caribbean and other communities.

Farrar argues persuasively that we need to learn a more nuanced language and analytic framework to understand the varieties of violent urban protest that are grouped under the term "riot" and considers what can be learned and reworked from scholarly attempts to place the event of "riot" in a larger social and historical context (Farrar 2009, pp. 103–118). Yet, even these attempts to place unrest in a wider context of ongoing social relations can tend towards stock explanations. If we decide that the significance of events cannot be discerned through attention to uniquely remarkable incidents, then the longer contextual narratives veer towards the stories that have already been told. In Britain, this can mean that riots are about race — and, conversely, the street unrest of markedly white groups, say in relation to football, is not a "riot".

A painful demonstration of these racialised codings was seen in the patterns of sentencing following disturbances in Bradford in 2001. Here, the proposal to allow the British National Party to march through predominantly Asian neighbourhoods of Bradford led to local resistance, with young Asian men occupying their local streets as a mark of self-defence. Disturbances followed in both Asian and white neighbourhoods, with animosity directed towards the police, yet only Asian men were charged under the terms of "riot" and given the disproportionately long sentences that are enabled by that definition of disorder. White participants from neighbouring areas were charged with lesser offences under the rubric of public order (for more on the disturbances in Bradford, see Bagguley and Hussain).

The imaginative grouping of all disturbances occurring in that week in August as "riot" — from the wannabe rioters of facebook incitement to fairly contained disturbance in relatively prosperous neighbourhoods to organised looting in the centres of large cities — represented a move away from this more usual formulation of the riot as an always somehow racialised event. Oddly, one outcome of the summer of 2011 is this small crack in the fictions of whiteness, as the revelation of multi-ethnic (and multi-generational) participation shifted the formulation of riot to become an (bad and undesirable) example of multi-ethnic co-existence, one opposed against a model of the good society as distinctly diverse yet united in the respectable defence of property and public order. The rapid polarisation of Britain's already highly divided society under the coalition government has expanded the category of people who do not count, or are not deserving of respect (or benefits), or are to be considered less than citizens. Paradoxically, this process threatens to unsettle the marginalisation of the racialised, because now, many others are vilified for different reasons and yet through similar methods and means.

Broken Britain and the Regionalisation of Unrest

The widespread anxiety about the meaning of the riots quickly and predictably becoming a metaphor for a wider unease about something amiss in British society. Much earlier, and to some controversy, Cameron had suggested that we were living in a broken Britain. This phrase was coined, no doubt after extensive research and refinement, to reflect both the renewed caring aspect of the Tories under Cameron and the continuation of familiar conservative themes — family, discipline, order, and tradition. In common with some other coinages of the no longer nasty party under Cameron, the concept was underdeveloped, yet, unfortunately for critics, the sense that something was, indeed, broken seems to have struck a cord with the electorate. It was this moment of popular resonance that, inevitably, was resurrected in the face of the August riots. Rather than a tearing apart of the entire social fabric, my sense is that the brokenness of Britain was understood as a welcome recognition by the political class of a widespread perception that there has been a coarsening of everyday sociality that corrodes all of our lives (see Bhattacharyya, Cowles, Garner and Hussain 2012 for some discussion of this).

The consumption of the coverage of the riots as a kind of morality tale of our time was framed by this sense of coarsening, yet the character of the coarsening was seen to vary according to location. Regional characters emerge through the narrative of the "riots" — an episodic process that is told in a manner that echoes the nation's familiarity with soap opera and reality shows. In an echo of the regional types that have been embodied in both soaps and reality TV, the media representation of the disturbances also took on a regionalised character — or were understood to be filled with regional characters. Broadly, we could summarise the media telling of the week's events as:

London — so-called feral youth go on the rampage, using the incident of Mark Duggan's death as a pretext to loot.

Birmingham — the temporary lapse in order as the police fail to anticipate the pattern of disorder opens a space for allegedly longstanding tensions between minority ethnic groups to be played out violently in public space.

Manchester — the temporary lapse in order as the police fail to anticipate the pattern of disorder opens a space for organised crime to loot in a systematic manner, using local youth as both foot soldiers and sources of intelligence.

Liverpool, Nottingham — among other major conurbations that attracted less sustained national coverage, and instead functioned as indicators of national contagion and the uncovering of submerged dysfunction.

Accounts of each local incarnation focused on an aspect of the anxieties that have beset public debate in recent times, yet each also marked the simultaneous specificity of regional frames and the connectivity of a nation understood as an assemblage of dislocated yet synchronicitous events and experiences. In this imagining of nation as a collection of dysfunctional fragments that was united by a shared yet varied brokenness, it was possible to revisit more than one set of recent government preoccupations — chaotic families here, divided neighbourhoods there, a failure of responsibility all over.

Over the course of the week, coverage and debate also took on an episodic character. Not one unifying story of nation, but an emerging story of interconnected, yet distinct brokenness in each location.

Birmingham as the Space of Race

Somehow, and immediately, unrest in Birmingham was described as continuing a history of inter-ethnic unrest in the city. Channel 4 news, among the less sensationalist news outlets in Britain, framed its Birmingham coverage by referring to the history of inter-ethnic tensions in the city. The Daily Mail, characteristically, chose to be more explicit. At a time when most commentary sought to distinguish the disturbances of 2011 from those of 1981, on the basis that 1981 was an understandable response to the institutional racism of that time whereas now things were, we were told, much improved and 2011 rioters were too feral to kick against injustice anyway, the Mail suggested that, from 1981 to 2011, street disorder in Birmingham has been caused by animosity between minority ethnic groups, with neither police or the majority population anywhere to be seen.

> Winson Green is a five-minute drive from Handsworth, scene of notorious race riots in the 1980s.

> Some claim these were fuelled by a nationwide wave of uprisings in the wake of the 1981 Brixton riot. Other sources have suggested that the local black British felt aggrieved at the increase in Asian-owned businesses which were prospering in the area. (Seamark, 2011)

This is broken Britain as failed multiculturalism — always with a trace of Powellite hysteria. Sooner or later, the streets will flow with blood as a result of "mass" immigration — minorities may fight each other initially, but this is a portent of what is to come for the majority community. Birmingham, it seems, has come to represent the preoccupation with proving that racism is an affliction of all communities, not only the majority.

The depiction of Birmingham as a space of inter-ethnic tensions can be recouped into a wider narrative of the post-racial in our times. This may seem a strange claim — how can the reinterpretation of social unrest as, always and necessarily when in this place, a matter of race represent an aspect of post-racial thinking. Here, I am positioning the fiction of the post-racial as an explicit and highly interested riposte to the particular racialised thinking of critiques of racism. This is a version of the post-racial that does not present "race" as a fiction of the past — instead, in the manner of so much diversity talk, the suggestion is that "race" does not matter, because everyone is a racist, so everyone suffers and everyone is equal.

In response to the continuing and systematic disadvantage faced by many minority ethnic groups, spaces — such as Birmingham — play an important representational role. Here, we are shown what multi-ethnic living means — and the meaning is, invariably, that these people do it to themselves. Goldberg describes this take-up of critiques of racism as a method of silencing complaints of racism — because only racists keep banging on about race, we post-racial liberals know that race is a fiction (Goldberg 2008).

Despite the police killing of Duggan, a young black man who is yet to be shown to have been armed, despite considerable police energies spent in pursuit of this "justification"; despite the attempts to paint Duggan as the aggressor; despite the old-fashioned disrespect that kept the family waiting all day and all night when police knew that he was already dead; despite the systematic character assassination of Duggan after his death; despite all of these painfully familiar details of continuing and violent state racism, the insistent official refrain was that 2011 could not be about racism, because that is not an issue here any more. Perhaps the riots showed that we remained divided, but the very different convivial practices of looting or defending property were pointed to as proof that the divider was not race (Addley, Taylor, Domokos and Lewis 2011).

Broken Britain, Interracial Violence and Post-Racial Fantasies

In what follows, I consider this unexpected acknowledgement of a version of lived multiculturalism as the contemporary reality of much of urban Britain and the manner in which these seemingly unprecedented disturbances became an opportunity to both shift the terms of national belonging while reaffirming some very old racist exclusions.

In any story of nation, family plays an important role. Even in our mobile times, nation remains a story about blood and kinship, as well as more open tests of belonging such as shared spaces, practices and imaginations. In our more knowing times, the claims of blood and land can be hard to fix to urbanised populations, but nationhood can remain a powerful story of something shared. Perhaps we have returned to dreams of home and hearth with nation imagined as a cluster of domestic spaces — with a shared participation in recognisable rituals of family marking a commitment to a larger shared culture without need of any fantasy of national blood ties. The shift in political rhetoric from any address to citizens in favour of describing voters as those belonging to "hard-working families" seems to confirm this reliance on metaphors and mythologies of family in contemporary political life.

The Tragedies of Muslim Families

The quick embrace and celebration of the Jahan family — and their astonishing ability to transcend their own grief and reach out to calm others — referenced this sense of shared national identity through family life. The reshaping of recent racisms in Britain has needed, as usual, some navigation between contradictory standpoints. So, strong families are essential for national well-being and the alleged collapse of the family is at the root of unrest and ill-discipline among the young — yet at the same time, some communities are too regulated in their domestic arrangements, their families are too authoritarian, always threatening to edge into violence. We might argue that the elastic term, "family", does stretch from sustenance to companionship to abuse and violence. Yet, the demonisation of family as the mark of monstrosity for some, yet the badge of civilisation for others can create a tension in popular understanding.

Three young Asian men, Haroon Jahan, Abdul Musavir and Shazad Ali, were killed by a car in alleged hit-and-run incident in Winson Green, Birmingham. The incident took place during Ramadan, and many young Muslim men had been gathering in the streets in residential areas of Birmingham, both protecting property and meeting friends. In the hours immediately after the death of his son, Jahan became a national hero for seeking to calm tensions in the community, even at this time of immense grief.

It has been some time since we saw a Muslim family in a good light. The concept of loving Muslim fathers and sons has been overshadowed by the shrill hysteria in relation to the alleged dangers of Muslim masculinity. In part, such an identification with Jahan in particular (widespread across the nation, apparently) seems an occasion for hope. Parental grief, in this instance, could be communicated as a universally understood emotion. If Cameron had sought to articulate broken Britain through scolding, this was a brokenness of shared loss. Parenthood, once again, becomes one of the reference points that can transcend the barriers of class and race in divided Britain. The popular resonance of the Stephen Lawrence case was made possible, in part, by the persistence and visibility of Stephen's parents. Although many other families had campaigned for justice for loved ones — and many others continue to do so — there was something about that moment of family tragedy that was communicable to the nation as a whole, at least for a moment. We might consider the deaths of Haroon, Shazad and Ali as a similar moment of identification.

Yet, somehow this highly staged empathy — look at us, understanding the pain of bereaved Muslims — has served only to reconfirm the unhappy racial politics of Britain. Just as the momentary identification with athletes of migrant heritage during the Olympics is understood as an anomalous blip (because the consensus remains that migrants contribute little or nothing), equally the Jahan family was represented continually as an admirable anomaly.

Good Brummie, Bad Brummie

Before the disturbances of August 2011, Birmingham sought to depict key anniversaries of 1980s riots as an opportunity to show how far the city had come. While, in a strangely partial yet still damning retrospect, the year 1985 was portrayed as a time of uncontainable racial tension, poverty and disorder in the city, year 2010 is presented as a time of interracial harmony in the pursuit of greater shared prosperity (Varma 2010). Importantly, both as a reflection of the Tory-LibDem coalition that ran Birmingham until May 2012 and in terms of the wider shift away from state-centred approaches to fostering racial justice in favour of supposedly market-based solutions to problems of inequality, there is a denial that systematic racism continues to exist.

In fact, and although a version of official multiculturalism has been blamed for not only failing to address the inequalities of racist societies but also for creating further divisions and competition for the resources accompanying political patronage, the model of competition as a method of resolving issues of distribution and participation has become celebrated in British public life as the approach most likely to engage ethnically diverse communities.

This rhetoric of trusting the mechanism of the market to resolve all social ills is, of course, a feature of far larger phenomena of our time. The various shortcomings and outright failures of state bureaucracies are presented as another aspect of the failings of institutional analysis — injustice is not regarded as institutional or systematic and, therefore, these previous attempts to create institutional or systemic responses to unfairness are derided as misconceptions of their time. Instead, we are led to believe, entrepreneurialism is the new social cohesion and forward-looking individuals abandon backward group affiliations altogether.

Soon after the terrible events of August 2011, it began to be suggested that Jahan was able to reach out to other communities and, in particular, forge bonds with the Sikh community because he had lived in Slough. This oddly highlighted detail of personal biography was considered an explanation for (unexpected) good Muslim behaviour.

It seems that in the national imagination, Birmingham figures as both a frightening portent of what is to come (if we do not control this dangerous multiculturalism in action) and as a kind of display of atavistic non-evolution. Of course, we are led to understand that these two aspects are connected. In a partial update of Roy Jenkins famous justification of immigration control, here it is only those who live with not too much diversity who can evolve and come to appreciate the post-racial pleasures of diversity. Slough might allow a person to crawl into modernity — Birmingham freezes inhabitants in the habits of racial division that belong to another age. In an echo of Mamdani's account of the conception of good and bad Muslims, civilised goodness must come from demonstrating an ability not to be constrained by ethnic or religious affiliation, to prove that, unlike those barbaric others of your type, you can be open to all others of all kinds (Mamdani 2004). The ability to display cosmopolitan consciousness becomes a requirement for those wishing to be regarded as human — the defence of property, a much celebrated activity in other locations during the riots, is not sufficient. This seemed to be understood by other bystanders, who also did their best to assert the cosmopolitan humanness of the dead boys and their families,

> Local resident Mohammed Shakiel said: 'They lost their lives for other people, doing the job of the police.

> They weren't standing outside a mosque, a temple, a synagogue or a church — they were standing outside shops where everybody goes. They were protecting the community as a whole. (Seamark 2011)

Here, the response is to the unspoken suggestion that young Asian men in the street were motivated by communal and exclusionary sentiments — that community defence could mean only the most narrowly understanding of community and that ethnic and religious identity overrides all other human connections for these poor people still stuck in the morass of race. This, after all, has been described consistently as the disease that mars the population of Birmingham.

A range of voices did seek to register disquiet at the depiction of Birmingham as a place defined by communal conflict. Sometimes, this was an explicit retort to the accusation of broken Britain, as in Jahan's formulation of a nation of "good people",

> Despite everything that happened, he won't accept politicians' rhetoric that we live in a "broken society". He speaks of the sense of unity that drew 35,000 people to Haroon's funeral. "It was amazing," he says. "It was beautiful. It made me respect the public even more. There are a lot more good people than there are bad people ... but unfortunately the bad people find a way into our lives a lot easier. (Bignell 2011)

Others argued that it was only (male) minorities of a certain generation who could overcome the brokenness and coarsening that had overtaken British society. After more than a decade in which the Muslim man became the most widely vilified transnational enemy of all things western, here authoritarianism becomes orderliness and social conservatism becomes citizenship again,

> Having seen both sides of the proverbial coin these men are fiercely protective of their adopted homeland. They cherish the stability and the peaceful lives they are able to live. It makes them proud to be British. In some instances, more so than their children who are born here. It is noticeable that the actions of some hardline young Muslims who turn to fundamentalist teachings are almost always at odds with the views of their parents, many of whom have seen less fortunate times.
>
> I experienced this personally when as a conflicted teenager I adopted a deeply anti-British stance, much to the disapproval of my father. My dad would often say: "You'll realise one day how fortunate you are that this is your home." (Hanif 2011)

Once again, we are offered a version of the good Muslim — here grateful migrants who value the freedoms of liberal democracy — but always as a counterpoint to the accusation that there are still too many bad Muslims undoing the contribution of these valued but quiet (untroublesome, older) men.

It could be remarked that Jahan does not appear to be a first-generation migrant nor did he seek to profess his allegiance to any particular incarnation of nationhood. However, his intervention and continuing conduct was incorporated into many accounts of the "real meaning of Britishness" or the real meaning of community — he attracted admiration as a result of demonstrating what British Muslims could be, but, the strong implication remained, on the whole were not.

Good and Bad Muslims Again

Among the more bizarre commentaries on the Winson Green deaths was the comparison made by Julie Birchall. In a piece purportedly commemorating 9/11, Burchill delivered a cartoon denunciation of extremism while arguing that men of peace would win out — men of peace such as Tariq Jahan and Barack Obama. The celebration of Jahan followed the script established in other commentaries — the ability to show magnanimity in the face of huge personal loss, the reaching out to others, the plea for peace — yet, here, these virtues were compared with the assassination of Osama Bin Laden and, oddly, the ability of Obama to remain nonchalant and casually dressed through this operation ("Dressed with the casualness of a delivery man among the suited, booted and military-medal-heavy Anglo-Saxon types … no pretensions to him at all. As the Navy Seals stormed Bin Laden's Pakistani fortress, the President watched stony-faced, before turning to the room and saying simply: "We got him".). For Burchill, Jahan's actions had managed to redeem Islam in the eyes of a world that she describes as legitimate in its attacks on Muslims,

> JUST one month before the tenth anniversary of the 9/11 massacre, one man did something which went a good way towards making up for a decade in which Islam appeared the most serious threat to world peace since the Nazis were vanquished more than 65 years ago'. (Burchill, 2012)

Her account, written as always for entertainment and outrage, sought to link the forgiveness of Tariq Jahan with the vengeance of Barack Obama,

> But justice is as important as forgiveness, and in May this year, another man — not as noble and selfless a man as Tariq Jahan, but a good man nevertheless — put wheels of vengeance, rather than clemency, in motion. (Burchill 2012)

The logic of the good Muslim — and the accompanying implication that we have all been living under the shadow of the spectre of the bad Muslim — demands that the performance of difference and distance from those other bad Muslims continues endlessly. Vengeance can be over in a murderous moment, forgiveness is a lifetime's slog where any slip can prove again that there are no good Muslims. As we have learned before, the burden of representation is pretty heavy and hard to hold steady,

> What makes Jahan, a delivery driver born in Slough to immigrants from India and Pakistan, such an unlikely British hero is that he is a British Muslim. As a

friend of the family told me: "This was the week Muslims, Asians and Pakistanis everywhere were liberated. Thanks to Tariq, we're all seen in a different light now — not in a negative light, not just as terrorists". (Hasan 2011)

2012

In August 2012, eight men were cleared of all charges relating to the deaths of Haroon Jahan, Shazad Ali and Abdul Musavir. While others had been given custodial sentences for crimes, such as stealing a bottle of water, a packet of sweets or a single trainer (without the other half of the pair) or for receiving an item of stolen goods as a present, no one was sentenced to a single day of prison time for the deaths of these three men.

Birmingham remains marked as a space of potential interracial violence — the 2012 trial was reported primarily in terms of the possibility of inter-community conflict in the aftermath of any verdict and, once again, the Jahan family was called upon to embody the admirable anomaly that forsakes vengeance.

In the post-Olympics glow, Britain congratulates itself on having forged a liveable and non-embarrassing version of everyday nationhood, one that might be, finally, at ease with the diversity of the actual, not imagined, population. Yet, it is still for others to prove that they can remain good Muslims (or good black men or good asylum-seekers) rising above the day-to-day injustice of our times to prove that they can belong through an endless trial of forgiveness. Perhaps this is a kind of lived conviviality, but at what price?

References

Addley, E., Taylor, M., Domokos, J. & Lewis, P. (2011) 'UK Riots: Those who Seek to Racialise this Problem are Taking us Backwards', http://www.guardian.co.uk/uk/2011/aug/10/uk-riots-racial dimension?intcmp=239 (accessed 10 August 2011).

Bagguley, P. & Hussain, Y. (2008) *Riotous Citizens: Ethnic Conflict in Multicultural Britain*, Ashgate, Aldershot.

Bhattacharyya, G., Cowles, J., Garner, S., & Hussain, A. (2012) Communities, Centres, Connections, Disconnections: Some Reflections on the Riots in Birmingham, socresonline February 2012, http://www.socresonline.org.uk/17/1/11.html

Bignell, P. (2011) 'Tariq Jahan: Overcome by the Kindness of Strangers', *Independent newspaper*, http://www.independent.co.uk/news/people/profiles/tariq-jahan-overcome-by-the-kindness-of-strangers-2360516.html (accessed 25 September 2011).

Billig, M. (1995) *Banal Nationalism*, Sage: London.

Burchill, J. (2012) 'Extremists Love Death. We Love Life. Brave Men as Different as TariqJahan and Barack Obama Mean Life will Surely Win', http://www.thesun.co.uk/sol/homepage/news/september11/3810598/Extremists-love-death-We-love-life-Brave-men-as-different-as-Tariq-Jahan-and-Barack-Obama-mean-life-will-surely-win.html#ixzz25bByJSBD (accessed 13 September 2011), http://www.thesun.co.uk/sol/homepage/news/september11/3810598/Extremists-love-death-We-love-life-Brave-men-as-different-as-Tariq-Jahan-and-Barack-Obama-mean-life-will-surely-win.html

Doyle, J. (2010) 'Binge-drinking Violence 'Creating no-go Areas', *Independent newspaper*, http://www.independent.co.uk/news/uk/politics/bingedrinking-violence-creating-nogo-areas-1872288.html (accessed 19 January 2010).

Farrar, M. (2009) 'Violent Urban Protest – Identities, Ethics and Islamism (2009)', in Bhattacharyya, G. (ed.) *Ethnicities and Values in a Changing World*, Ashgate, Farnham, pp. 103–118.

Fraser, C. (2010) 'France Hit by New Wave of Strikes over Pension Reforms', http://www.bbc.co.uk/news/world-europe-11570828

Goldberg, D. (2008) *The Threat of Race: Reflections on Racial Neo-Liberalism*, Blackwell, Oxford.

Hanif, F. (2011) 'Tariq Jahan's is the Patriotic Voice of a First-generation Muslim Migrant', *Guardian Comment is Free*, http://www.guardian.co.uk/commentisfree/2011/aug/11/tariq-jahan-first-generation-muslim-migrant (accessed 11 August 2011).

Hasan, M. (2011) Tariq Jahan tells Mehdi Hasan: 'I don't see a broken society', *The New Statesman*, 24 Aug.

Jeffries, S. (2012) 'Has London 2012 got us all Blubbing? I Second that Emotion', *Guardian*, http://www.guardian.co.uk/sport/london-2012-olympics-blog/2012/aug/03/london-2012-olympics-blubbing-emotion (accessed 3 August 2012).

Maltezou, R. & Papachristou, H. (2011) 'Greek Police Battle Rioters as Austerity Bill Passed', http://www.reuters.com/article/2011/06/29/us-greece-parliament-idUSTRE75S70J20110629

Mamdani, M. (2004) *Good Muslim, Bad Muslim, Islam, the USA, and the Global War Against Terror*, Permanent Black, Delhi.

Seamark, M. (2011) 'Grieving Father's Voice of Sanity: As 'Race Murder' of Three Young Asians Sends Riot City to Boiling Point, Man who Lost Son Calls for Calm', http://www.dailymail.co.uk/news/article-2024375/BIRMINGHAM-RIOTS-Race-murder-victim-Haroon-Jahans-father-Tariq-calls-calm.html#ixzz25b2Hww4d (accessed 11 August 2011).

Tremlett, G. (2012) 'Spain's Indignado Protesters Mark Anniversary of Anti-austerity Rallies', *Guardian newspaper*, http://www.guardian.co.uk/world/2012/may/13/spain-indignado-protesters-anniversary-rallies (accessed 13 May 2012).

Varma, A. (2010) 'Handsworth Riots 25 Years on: How Regeneration Helped to Heal the Wounds', *Birminhgam Post*, http://www.birminghampost.net/news/west-midlands-news/2010/09/10/handsworth-riots-25-years-on-how-regeneration-helped-to-heal-the-wounds-65233-27245161/ (accessed 10 September 2010).

Contexts for Distraction

Tom Henri and John Hutnyk

This paper discusses the events of August 2011 through our reading of a series of reports and responses by academics and commentators. These are critically and collectively evaluated as lacking in so far as we see the deployment of gang-talk, the promotion of role models, narrow-cast notions of race and platitudes about the justice system as a distraction from wider issues. Providing context for "reading" the riots/uprisings, we suggest that, at stake in each case, we see the limits of a scholarly commentary that remains unprepared to address the conflict and turmoil of "Big Society" austerity thinking.

This paper is a critical response to both the events of the popular uprisings of August 2011, which have come to be known as the London Riots,[1] and the subsequent research, policy and media outputs of various institutionally based reporters, analysts and academics in the year that has followed. We examined a range of texts to identify rhetorical devices that we refer to collectively as a set of diversionary and attention-distracting "Jedi mind tricks".[2] That is, we argue that a variety of commentators on the uprisings deploy a series of media-biased psych-operations or sleights-of-hand in the construction of an apologetic popular discourse on the events of August 2011. These diversionary devices could be constructed as distractions from both the meanings and implications of the disturbances, which would otherwise be obvious and more widely recognised. Hence, these are "mind tricks". We use a phrase derived from the well-known intergalactic ideological practice, associated with clerical

---

1. Not only in London of course, but tourism authority branding belies the spread to nearly every city in England in the days after the first night in Tottenham.
2. In Star Wars Episode IV: A New Hope armed storm troopers searching the planet Tatooine for "droids" (robots) are sent on their way by Obi Wan Kenobi (Alec Guinness), using his superior mental control of "the force". It is our contention that a similar, but much diminished, mode of distraction operates in the search for "explanations" of the August riots in the UK in 2011. From David Cameron's electorate-pandering declarations of a war on gangs, to the more nuanced insistence of organisations like the Centre for Social Justice that his policy "is not working" (Centre for Social Justice, 2012) and even in the respected *Guardian*/LSE research reports or the works of philosopher-pundits like Slavoj Zizek, the effort to explain away the uprising deserves a more critical eye.

force and power, because often the ruse of "commentary" is used to conceal and obscure significance and to provide legitimacy for reactionary politics.

The distractions we identify here include more obvious moves such as employment of insecurities about class and race to push a security agenda, and stereotyping of class positions and racial profiles. There is also a trick of the market which casts the evil of "shopping with violence" as a rhetorical application that obscures deeper insecurities about consumption. Another trick pushes an "austerity discourse" which relies upon identifying "rioters" in ways that psychologise and pathologise participants in the uprising. This ploy has the capacity to simultaneously confirm *and* obscure the political trick *and* the market trick. Such deceptions reorient our attention from critiques of the structural conditions of the uprisings, and blinker our capacity to consider the political legitimacy of those involved. In the aftermath of the uprisings, we have identified a further "trick" that belongs to the otherwise socially validated and institutionally credentialised field of socio-cultural research; studies of the disturbances focus upon individualised "instances" that "illustrate" — for readers — the condition of "the poor" and mark out an abstract austerity as unexamined antecedent and context. We argue that this works as a partial justification for the exploitation system of wage labour and class hierarchy in a stagnant, recessionary economy. In a rough-sketch "austerity-discourse" that disguises any urgent political consideration, the trope of "the poor" is defined, promoted and maintained by the ruling class as an excuse for interventionist palliative "care". The ruling class are self-defined in terms of their relationship with the poor as sometimes benevolent sometimes exasperated providers of understanding and policy, such that understanding *away* the material conditions of this "poor" in relation to the well-off, and the "squeezed middle", means all causes and consequences of August 2011 can be recast as a need for "policy initiatives", and further austerity. We see this as belonging to a deeply hierarchical history that has not denied its imperial past, so much as recast it in renditions of the old divide and rule that served so well at home and abroad. We see various manifestations of a defence of this ideology in otherwise well-meaning analysts who themselves promise to offer "better" understandings, and "deeper" reasonings. It is our view that such rhetorical sleights-of-hand feed into a grander trick; which is the trick of the UK coalition government policy agenda known as the Big Society. We will argue that the Big Society trick is about the dismantling of social infrastructure in ways that undermine hard fought-for, and as yet incomplete, frameworks of social solidarity, civic opportunity and multicultural redress. In place of State responsibility, it leaves people with a pared down set of "community involvement" tools for neo-Darwinian minimal survival in a period of imposed and unwarranted austerity.[3] Clearly the Big Society is not the sole component

---

3. Scott Lash, speaking at a student run Centre for Cultural Studies event at Goldsmiths College in October 2010 had already pointed out that the austerity cuts were unnecessary, that the deficit shortfall was comparatively small, that the cuts were politically motivated, and that something more than cant was needed (from memory, Hutnyk).

of the dysfunctional capitalism that gives us recession, stagflation and austerity, and we do not have direct one-to-one equations that show BS as responsible for the disturbances of August 2011, nor would we say Tory policy is a consequence of the uprisings. We do insist, however, that "the riots" provided a useful screen upon which the sitting Government projects a view of the world that puts the onus of social policy back onto communities and localities while withdrawing State subsidy in the interests of corporate privilege. This is a core part of an agenda of neo-liberal flexiblisation, casualisation and lumpenisation which benefits the increasing accumulation of capital for the super-elite.

Distraction has quite an epidemiology. We identify several contexts that should be remembered as the wider scenario in which the action of August 2011 took place. These include a long history of proletarianisation and degradation of conditions for the employed, part-time, under- and unemployed workers of the UK, increasingly difficult work conditions, longer work hours, widening pay gap, and uncertainty as to opportunities, including those in training and education, increasingly vocationalised with low prospects and bleak outlook. Also a long history of race-based inequality of opportunity, under-investment in certain oft-mentioned "problem" areas, the twin scourges of gentrification and urban blight, a north—south divide in both capital and country, and a surveillance system on the streets that highlights and enforces this inequity. Ostensibly the trigger — uncomfortable pun intended — was the shooting to death of Mark Duggan in Tottenham, itself belonging to a long history of extra-juridical Police executions that shame the failure of the Independent Police Complaints Commission to prosecute any of those 1000+ UK police killings[4] that reach across a tragic litany of names of the dead. Violent policing in the UK is only one side of an even wider global violence that involves geopolitical intrigue, imperial wars and neo-colonial reaction, divide and rule. The brutal history of capital abroad — a "history written in annals of blood and fire" Marx calls it (1867/1976, p. 875) — reaches right up to present-day wars in Afghanistan, Iraq, Palestine, Somalia and returns to the metropolitan streets as a low-level everyday anxiety about the "War on Terror", which itself has its own differential impact, especially upon Muslims and anyone who might look suspicious, such as the Brazilian passenger on a tube in Stockwell in 2005.[5] The

---

4. See the film *Injustice*, 2001 Dir Ken Fero and Tariq Mehmood, and the website of Family and Friends United. In 2011 UFF reported: "The Independent Advisory Panel on Deaths in Custody report published in 2011 stated: in total, there were 5,998 deaths recorded for the 11 years from 2000 to 2010. This is an average of 545 deaths per year" See http://uffc-campaigncentral.net/2012/06/national-fathers-day-vigils-make-a-mark/ retrieved July 27 2012. The list of the Institute for Race Relations, maintained by Harmit Ahrwal, provides equally appalling reading: http://www.irr.org.uk/news/black-deaths-in-custody/ - retrieved July 27 2012.

5. Jean Charles de Menezes was shot multiple times in the head on a tube carriage in Stockwell after being trailed by surveillance police under the watch of Commander Cressida Dick. The only charge brought against this action — a daytime murder of a Londoner without cause — was one of a danger to public health and safety. Those charged were acquitted and Cressida Dick was awarded the Queen's Police Medal for distinguished service — BBC News December 31, 2009 - http://news.bbc.co.uk/1/hi/england/london/8435507.stm — retrieved August 17 2012.

Terror trick leaves all residents subject to a low-level surveillance anxiety which itself has become commodified in the CCTV-driven security State.[6]

Another context for August 2011 is of course the sometimes more promising, but not always positively resolved, wider series of global uprisings that follow from Tunisia in 2010, Egypt 2011, and in differing ways, the NATO intervention in Libya, the Indignados, or "15 M Movement", of Madrid and even the student protests in London in November and December 2010. We, however, would also recognise that listing contexts can readily become a trickster device in an article such as this. We list them and expect them to expand since the uprisings are the prism of interest for so many today, and continuing. That said, if we hold any deeper examination of such wider "contexts" in abeyance we would like to start from the premise that, despite the omniscience of so many Jedi-like analysts and their abundant commentary, there has not yet been, and perhaps cannot yet be, any clear single narrative of the events that lead up to, or from, August 2011.[7] Certainly the contest of interpretations where everything from flashpoints of individual emotion — of which we keep to ourselves[8] — through to pervasive and invasive imbrications of global capital flows, finance, strategy and control, does not yet make up a coherent picture that we would happily rest and accept. We see instead a sequence of interested and careerist moves to provide excuses, scapegoats and misdirection. The explanations proposed by some politicians, academics, media pundits, the police and even celebrities share more as rhetorical devices than they do as frames for insight and further action.[9] Nevertheless, we insist — mind trick alert — that there are points of convergence where quite different specific narratives deal with otherwise similar themes and thus feed into a smaller number of meta-narratives relating to looting, gangs, policing and juridico-legal practices. As we clarify these narrower codifications, the point is that these again serve to deceive us and obscure the operations of capital and the deeper significance of the uprisings for all involved.

---

6. Elsewhere, one of us has written about this as a Pantomime Terror, see: Hutnyk 2011.
7. Our examination of self referential commentaries as merely promotional is not an anti intellectual position, so much as it is an attempt to question the ways in which intellectual positions, including claims for more and better analysis, are often left unexamined as regards the privilege of making, or at least publishing, any analysis at all. We have no illusions that our own work is also subject to a certain privilege.
8. The Wildcat group offer the observation that "Comment on subjective factors should be left exclusively to the subjects in question, although this right has already been usurped by countless social ventriloquists. The most it is possible to say here is that some members of a class subjected to intensive and invasive management refused at specific times and in various ways to be managed or manageable" in "Detest and Survive", http://www.wildcat-www.de/en/actual/DETEST_AND_SURVIVE.html — retrieved August 17 2012
9. We note the provocative critique of an earlier uprising, in 1982, that was helpfully republished in 2008: "The riots at least should prove a lucrative source of income for that symposium of oily rags. The Sociology of Deviancy (Wolfie Smith, Speed, Tucker and June, 1982) http://www.revolt-againstplenty.com/index.php/recent/34-archivelocal/37-like-a-summer-with-a-thousand-julys — retrieved 16 August 2012

Political Gangs

One of the first and most obvious tricks deployed by the political class was to blame the events of the first few nights of August 2011 on gangs. The British Prime Minister David Cameron, used a speech just days after the disturbances to announce he was declaring "a concerted, all-out war on gangs and gang culture" (Cameron 2011a). Politicians have long been partial to declaring war on nebulous concepts ever since J. Edgar Hoover declared a "War on Crime" in the 1930s, as part cover for an anti-communist crusade that led to the House Un-American Activities Commission and the red-baiting of progressive film makers (no HUAC, no Star Wars, no Jedi). The ever-reliable bogeyman Richard Nixon declared a "War on Drugs" in 1971, which then became code for a military push into first Asia (see McCoy 2009) and especially under Ronald Reagan, into South America (see Vidal 2002). Other declarations of war sound more or less positive, but also turn out to have a dubious provenance — Lyndon B Johnson in 1964 declared "War on Poverty" so as to cash-in on the legacy of Kennedy and Roosevelt, and Indira Gandhi also declared "War on Poverty" — though in her case, it was *garibi hatau*, more literally "eradicate poverty", and was in effect a campaign cover for the electoral fraud which eventually had her suspended from running in elections for six years (Chatterjee 1997).

The "War on Gangs" of course also has a cinematic bent, and involves the same sorts of cover stories, demonisations and distractions, as well as a guilty romanticisation — if we think of James Dean and Marlon Brando as rebel youth "without a cause", any wider contextualisation of "youth" alienation is abandoned in the distraction and terror occasioned by motorcycles and leather. Brando and Dean serve to divert attention from social dissatisfaction amongst post-war Americans at the time of the "Police Action" in Korea and the early days of the Cold War. Fifty years later in the UK, gesturing to his Conservative Party base, the British leader's gang-war talk belongs to a similar social profiling. As Cameron and his advisors are surely aware — and indeed, this is just why it is politically convenient for them — the concept of the gang, or rather the concept of a gang *of the young and poor*, has so often played a role in the construction of troubled youth, fear of others and deviance that it is beyond cliché (see Cohen & Young 1981). In old social learning and differential association theory, the more "deviants" are labelled deviant, the more likely they are to "be" deviant (Sykes & Matza 1993). Also implicit in the use of the term "gang" is a potent projection of the nihilism to be associated with anti-social working-class sensibilities, from football violence (see John King, *The Football Factory, England Away* etc[10]) to London's perceived knife-crime epidemic.[11]

---

10. John King's novels on football in England in the 1990s perhaps offer the best ethnography of contemporary Britain available today.
11. Is Britain in the grip of a knife crime epidemic? http://www.telegraph.co.uk/news/uknews/1572908/Is-Britain-in-the-grip-of-a-knife-crime-epidemic.html retrieved 29th August 2012.

Our argument here is that ideas about youth, the poor and criminality congeal around bogus notions of gang activity alongside anti-social behaviour and the demonisation of working class families. As Mccarthy observes:

> From judgements about the status of families living on council estates, the conduct of "irresponsible" parents, to the "anti-social" actions of lower class young people, there is a certain repetitive cycle of anxieties about forms of class culture which are deemed "bad", "wrong", or in need of "correction" (Mccarthy 2011, p. 495).

Journalist, Owen Jones takes this argument further to opine that the anti-social behaviour agenda has;

> [...] increased the bad reputation of young working-class kids and popularized the chav caricature (O. Jones 2011, p. 95).

Although the ASBO was a New Labour project, this mode of control has in many ways been extended by the Con-Dem Coalition. We do not think it a coincidence that New Labour's ASBO-advocate and "Respect" czar, Louise Casey is now advising David Cameron in the wake of the "riots".[12] She is "tasked this time with fixing the chaotic families of 'Broken Britain'".[13] What is amazing here is the "intervention" Casey proposes will target the most "disruptive and chaotic" families with a "full family" perspective that combines traditional services and crisis management — drug use, domestic violence — with better parenting classes, and treatment for the "unexpected" problem of arson. Casey's report is based on interviews with just 16 "troubled families", but the project she heads will expand exponentially to "get underneath the skin" of 12,000 such families (Casey 2012, p. 3).

Proletarian gangs are often portrayed as a kind of infection of the social body, as amoral and destructive, whereas the amoral-yet-sophisticated mannered destruction of bourgeois gangs such as the Bullingdon Club convey a different class and culture aesthetic enabled by privilege. Both Cameron, the future British Prime Minister, and Boris Johnson, the future Mayor of London, each coming to power not long before the uprisings of August, were members of the "Buller" in 1987. Significant wealth is required to gain access to the Bullingdon Club, and members of the club are known for engaging a range of violent behaviours and having little regard for other people's property or the law (Pickard 2010). "What's all this then?", a pantomime policeman might be made to ask. We are tempted to say, along with Obi Wan from *Star Wars*: "these are not the rioters you are looking for; they can go about their business". When pressed by the BBC's Evan Davis on the similarities between the

---

12. "Riots: Louise Casey — Blair's respect tsar - to aid PM" BBC News September 7, 2011 - http://www.bbc.co.uk/news/uk-politics-14819727 — retrieved August 4 2012.
13. "Louise Casey's troubled families programme ignores the real problem; Patrick Butler, Guardian July 18, 2012, - http://www.guardian.co.uk/society/2012/jul/18/louise-casey-troubled-families-problem — retrieved August 28 2012.

violent behaviour of the Bullingdon club as a gang associated with violence, and the behaviour of young people involved in rioting and looting the Prime Minister replied, "We all do stupid things when we are young and we should learn the lessons" (Cameron 2011b). A far cry from Cameron's assessment of the behaviour of young people involved in the riots as, "criminality, pure and simple ... it has to be confronted and defeated" (Cameron 2011c). Despite a sociological tradition of critical teaching that warns against such bad habits, it is nevertheless the case that the code word "gang" is read in middle Britain as synonymous with black youth, knives, guns and drugs.[14] The standard fears see many different commentaries portraying groups of black young people as dangerous, sanctifying the sartorial aesthetic of the hoody as a marker of violence and enacting racially-biased policing tactics such as Section 43 of the Terrorism Act 2000. All this marks being young and black as synonymous of danger. It is not a mere quirk of urban life that the Metropolitan Police Service of London stops and searches nearly 10,000 people a year under Section 43 and Section 60 of the Public Order Act 1994 (Van Bueren & Woolley 2010). The majority of these people are black and Asian young men, yet not one person stopped under this section has been charged or convicted of terrorism or a terror-related offence. We see this racialisation of perceived youth violence used by a number of commentators to undermine support for multicultural settlement, as rendered in accusations of "sleepwalking to segregation" (Phillips 2005) through to the stunning hypocrisy of blaming others for making Britain a soft target for terrorism (Prins & Salisbury 2008).

Race, Control

Despite what the Khalid Qureshi Foundation and Chelsea Ives Youth Centre have called "a thousand slurred treatises on the concept of the gang" (Mute 2011, p. 104), we note that some found it difficult to be put off by the lack of evidence of gang-involvement, for example the Governments' own report, "After the Riots" offers from its "Communities and Victims Panel":

> While we know that most of the convicted rioters were not gang members, *we also know* that gangs operate in a large number of areas where the riots occurred. Some young people are exposed to imagery and attitudes associated with gang culture from an early age, which glamorizes a life of criminality outside the system and which eschews any empathy for the victims of crime (Singh 2012, p. 49 — our italics).

The report then continues to use the lack of gang evidence as a conjuring trick to deny the hierarchical and racist context of the uprisings. Take, for example,

---

14. Many references here are possible here, one worth reading is the Khalid Qureshi Foundation and Chelsea Ives Youth Centre text "Riot Polit-Econ" in the *Mute* special issue "Well the first thing I want to say is, politics my arse" (*Mute* Volume 3 # 2, 2011–12).

the juxtaposition of these two sentences; "We do not believe that these were race riots. Most of the convicted rioters were not gang members." (Singh 2012, p. 25). Surely, the question to ask is how can there only be a racial-aspect to the events if gangs were involved? The equation here is that race signifies gangs in some one-to-one correspondence, but the escape clause shows the commentators as not-racist because they explicitly disavow a focus upon gangs. Actually, much was made on all sides of the gang "armistice" which lasted for four days. Showing the convoluted logic that a taboo on even talking of race is actually the preserve of racists, a closer look at language reveals this. A year after the uprisings, despite the "evidence", the Guardian's "crime correspondent" was able to report that "members of different gangs ... had put aside their differences" and "run amok" (Laville 2012, p. 10). The expression "run amok" has its provenance in colonial era fears of wild insurgency in the Malay Peninsula, and thereby without mentioning the lost Empire, introduces again the underpinnings of an unexamined white supremacy that reaches from colonial narrative through to the deep ruling-class anxieties of the contemporary police state.

There are, however, contexts in which proletarian youth can join gangs and engage in violence as legitimised and mandated forms of state power. It is a different kind of war on poverty, more like a war of impoverished thinking, that gives us the War on Terror. The close link between coercion and limited opportunities means that we see some young people joining the Police, or even the armed forces so as to fight in theatres of little strategic importance to their lives. Conflicts hatched amongst cabals such as those analysts of Weapons of Mass Destruction, agents of the demonisation of Muslims and the "Islamic threat" — rely upon the close-nit gang ethos called nationalism. Off to war — on poverty, drugs, or crime: it surely is the case that some youth join the army because regimented life provides their only viable means of escape from austerity — albeit with the associated risk of capture and violent death, or alternately, a role as torturer and facilitator of rendition, custody death and deportation. We note this also because in the Big Society context of the defunding of Higher Education in the UK, military sponsored education may, in the future, provide one of the few opportunities for poor young people to access tertiary places. It is no ironic accident the Conservative Government response to "disadvantage" is to deploy uniforms as a "gang" containment strategy — prison uniforms, police uniforms, army uniforms, scout uniforms, volunteer Olympic Ambassador shirts and hi-vis community service jackets as the pantomime dress-up versions of this only too real farce. In August 2012, the uniform-insanity went so far as to announce the deployment of Baden Powell's scout packs as final solution: "The traditionally middle-class, white youth clubs often found in leafy suburbs and shire counties but not in inner cities" will be deployed in 400 new sites to "provide 10,000 more places for disadvantaged youths, including offenders, disruptive schoolchildren, children in care and the unemployed ... the cash for "uniformed" groups suggest ministers prefer more disciplined associations over less-established local services" (Sherman 2012).

It has been our contention that the politicians' trick of evoking the spectre of the gang performed the neat sidestep of articulating a popular discourse regarding insecurities about class and race without having to acknowledge it as such. We think there is an operational distinction in place that renders chav delinquency as consequent upon faulty white working-class parents, with their allegedly inadequate parenting skills, need for support and Louise Casey-led "full family" social worker intervention, whereas knife-crime gangster activity implicates black youth with guns and drugs, and requires the deployment of police units, courts, community workers and jail. That the situation is always mixed does not undermine the argument that a racist distinction is made at the level of presentation and policy. All Cameron had to do was mention gangs, at no point did he even need to mention race in order to play the race card. His white supremacy and his ruling class economic privilege were secured nevertheless — with the help of course of the Police and the Courts, who rushed to action once the uprising left the depressed areas of Tottenham and Lewisham and moved, as it did on day three, to the more respectable enclave of Ealing. We clearly see how the UK Government and their media confederates invoked gang-fear in the immediate aftermath of August 2011. We have suggested that fears based on social class and race privilege influence political thinking without the same politicians ever having to utter the terms race and class. Deep historical patterns emerge again and again, reinforced with research and learned commentary as much as by policy initiatives reconstruction and "intervention" programmes.[15] No need for any acknowledgement that structural inequality based on material and social disadvantage combined with racial discrimination played a role in the events of August 2011, everyone knew what was under discussion, but no-one needed to call it.

Shopping with Violence

It is too easy to complain that "rioting" youth are merely obsessed with trainers and TVs. Rather, the insurrectionary youth seem to understand better than most what these goods are — theirs. They grasp the fetish character of commodities and the theft of property as time. In a radical way, the youth grasp, and break, the distinction between use value and exchange value. Comfortable and well-to-do neoliberals lived for years off rampant expropriation, but now as the homing pigeon of inevitable crisis heads towards their own homes with militant intent, and with them having mortgaged the future to short-term gain, they seem perversely ignorant of causes and afraid. The sorry spectacle has them rushing around the yard trying to shore up the fortress where their property, interests and profits must be defended with a bolstered repressive

---

15. That Louise Casey proposes an "intervention" programme for 12,000 anti-social families reminded us of the Australian Howard Government's spurious "Intervention" in outback Australia, best examined through the dark glass of Angela Mitropoulos in "Notes on the Frontiers and Borders of the Postcolony" (Mitropoulos 2007).

apparatus that secures the survival of some, and foreclosure for everyone else.[16]

Prioritising the needs of the market over other forms of social and economic life, as exposed over and again in the post-Lehman Brothers bank-bail-out double-dip recession world, leads inexorably to further abstract dominance of the principle of exchange-value and the pursuit of profit, and property, by any means. Dysfunctional support for the market means use-values, and quality of life, come second even in the very domain of privilege that thrives on the margins of mercantile commerce. "Shopping with violence" effectively decouples the commodity from its exchange value, and so this serves as one of the few instances where an insight that ruptures market exchange might undo the reification of commodities as exchange or use values and offer a new take on value and commerce.

Bizarrely, the official response to the issue of shopping with violence is to provide more opportunities to shop for goods that the disenfranchised lumpenised proletariat cannot afford. In the UK Government's report on how to respond to the riots — the authors make special reference for the need for more department stores. Noted for special attention is the chain John Lewis which in Liverpool contributes over £1000 a month to charity and has had "a significant impact on the revitalization of the town centre" (Singh 2012, p. 81). The Big Society charity agenda gains a cut-price publicity coup here, in a Government report, which of course is also a political showcase — yet another example of hypocrisy and diversion. Where in the report was any extended consideration of these economic underpinnings or context?

Surprisingly, the high-profile LSE/Guardian "Reading the Riots" report also eschews such context and offers a very low horizon of empirical interviews and reportage, itself almost tabloid, so that here too any wider contextualisation, even a wrong one, is ruled inadmissible. This is why we take umbrage with the ways the issue of destruction of property was framed. The stock-standard notion is that those involved in the destruction were destroying their own communities and therefore not playing by the rules of the Big Society and, conversely, those who lost property in the disturbances or helped in the clean—up are champion role models with the required resolve to "get the community back on its feet". In the days immediately after the uprising, the press made much of the destruction of petit-bourgeois family-run businesses. The flagship case of this was the House of Reeves furniture store in Croydon, so iconic in that town that the area is known as "Reeves Corner". The Reeves family store had been on the site for 144 years before it was destroyed in a fire on the 8th August 2011. Much has been made of how this act of arson involved the perpetrator attacking his own community, and the correlate of this line involved eulogies applauding the determination of the owners to rebuild — a show of gumption for which, one year later, Nick Clegg, the Deputy Prime

---

16. If we must invoke the science fiction scenario of the sub-prime financial crisis, let it be through the work of Angela Mitropoulos (2012).

Minister, invited the Reeves to the London Olympics closing ceremony.[17] A non-points-scoring political response would be to insist on community service for the arsonist, not a photo-opportunity for Clegg rewarding the victims with hard-to-get tickets. A wider context is that the cycle of urban regeneration relies upon a longer-term pattern of running down of city areas until the timely intervention of developer capital and Government "reconstruction" — of which the boosterism of the London Olympics is the just the latest example. The Reeves family store is the shop-front display for a bigger project.

In this context, the action-shot front-page photograph of a Polish migrant, Monika Konczyk, jumping from the burning building gained near ubiquitous coverage. Interviewed in the *The Sun*, Konczyk is cited as saying:

> It is not what I expected of the English. I have never seen anything like this in Poland. Polish people are hard-working and respectable. They believe in working for a living, not stealing from others. If you want nice clothes or a new TV, you don't smash shop windows and loot them — you work to pay for them (Willetts August 13th 2011).

We do not wish to be discourteous to the losses and stress endured by Messrs Reeves or Ms. Konczyk, rather our argument here is how their misfortune is used to bolster the rhetoric of the Big Society. The Reeves family pulled their own socks up to continue their business, Monica Konczyk is a hardworking migrant who "never missed a day" of work before "Monday night's terror" (Willetts 2011). The problem is that the presentation of these narratives — hard working community-"inspirations" and poundland-working low-wage Poles — supports the paring down of social policy to the level of the individual who will get on with things in whatever adversity. A Battle of Britain ethos, generalised for all — and Government, and the press, there to defend them in splendid, photogenic, isolation, subject to tabloid propaganda profile-opportunism and fifteen minutes of fame.

Courting Trouble

The process of furthering the demonisation and criminalisation of "deviant" youth has very real and profound consequences for all those residing in the UK, not just those identified as miscreant, deviant or anti-social. The legitimacy of representative democracy relies upon the idea of the separation of powers between the executive, the legislature and the judiciary. It is the checks and balances that occur from this separation of powers that are

---

17. "Nick Clegg invites owner of burnt down Croydon furniture store to Games closing ceremony" ITV News August 10 2012 - http://www.itv.com/news/2012-08-10/nick-clegg-invites-owner-of-burnt-down-croydon-furniture-store-to-games-closing-ceremony/ For Clegg's photo with the Reeves, see: "House of Reeves chairman Nick Cleggs guest to closing ceremony" in the Croydon Guardian August 14, 2012, http://www.croydonguardian.co.uk/news/9871819.Furniture_store_chairman_invited_to_Olympics_closing_ceremony/.

supposed to give the governed, however fragile, a sense of freedom from tyranny. We vote for a legislature, they arrange an executive, which they then hold to account; the judiciary tests the work of both bodies through the courts. However, in the aftermath of the uprisings of 2011, there was a unification of these powers that disrupted, possibly forever, the settlement of representative democracy in the UK.

On his return from that holiday to attend a COBRA meeting to respond to the unrest, and denounce the gangs, Prime Minister Cameron's statement from the steps of Downing Street, said,

> I have this very clear message to those people who are responsible for this wrongdoing and criminality: you will feel the full force of the law, and if you are old enough to commit these crimes you are old enough to face the punishment (Cameron 2011c).

One week after this statement a circular from Her Majesty's Courts and Tribunals Service instructed magistrates to disregard normal guidelines when sentencing those involved in the disturbances (Piper 2011). In fact, the custodial rate for those convicted of riot-related crimes was twice the 2010 average for those dealt with in the crown court and four-times the rate of custody for those dealt with in the magistrates' courts.[18] This statistic has two important resonances: first, it defies any attempt at pretence of the separation of legal powers, which has grave implications for the founding idea of British liberal democracy. The other aspect is that, as Singleton has demonstrated by analysing postcode information from court data, the majority of those convicted of riot-related offences were from the most deprived localities in the UK (Singleton 2011). We might therefore infer that the majority of the convictions were of impoverished persons, and thus by increasing the custody-rate, the executive-branch of the government has achieved the splendid result of further criminalising the lumpen poor. Again, we do not have to leave the green zone security enclave of the mainstream media to find heavy rotation renditions of another striking photograph, this time of a young man posing with a bag of "Tesco value" rice, which he had allegedly looted.[19] "Everything Must Go" was the Daily Mail's inflammatory headline — context is indeed everything, and so we can assume that if he has been arrested and convicted for the offence of looting this bag of rice in a riot he will have a much higher chance of receiving a custodial sentence than if he had merely shoplifted the same food item. We hardly need comment on the ideological dynamic at play in the sideshow of a

---

18. http://www.guardian.co.uk/news/datablog/2012/jul/04/riot-defendants-court-sentencing — retrieved August 9, 2012.
19. "London Riots: They Stole Everything" Daily Mail August 10, 2011 — http://www.dailymail.co.uk/news/article-2024012/LONDON-RIOTS-2011-They-stole-EVERYTHING-Enfield-Clapham-shops-stripped-bare.html — retrieved August 10, 2011 [the "alleged" is ours, for forms sake].

(white) millionaire's daughter led astray by black convicted coke dealer to think there is something amiss in using the courts for propaganda.[20]

It should be no surprise that our analysis leans towards the conclusion that the sentencing of those involved in the uprising was politically-motivated. Presumably, the discursive justification for a significant ramping-up of custody rates was strategic thinking that this would act as future deterrence. McGuire notes, from his meta-analysis of what works in preventing crime, that there is little evidence to support the deterrence hypothesis (Maguire 2004). Having read our Foucault, or been closely advised by those who have,[21] we feel we can largely discount deterrence as a credible explanation for the changes in sentencing that accompanied the uprisings. "Better" explanations of the increasing use of draconian sentencing may have to do with the security agenda that dominates political moves in the post September 11, 2001 civil liberties environment. Since August 2011, Britain has experienced a Royal wedding, a Royal jubilee and the Olympics and Paralympics and each of these events has been utilised to further securitise the nation in general and the capital specifically. In the year since the events of August 2011 there has been a significant increase on the already huge number of CCTV cameras in London, blast barriers have been installed in front of many more central London locations, the Police routinely patrol with automatic weapons and now we all know there are missile systems installed on the roofs of social housing in East London and in the parks of South East London. In some way, the riots provided a pretext for increasing the security and surveillance of the city and the state due to the exceptionality of the events, yet as with the militarisation of London, that — to be fair — has always been in process, the exceptionality of sentencing soon becomes the norm.

On the other hand, we assume that increased security and militarisation may also breed further dissent just as much as it will ensure compliance. We note that it was very clear the Police were on the back foot for four days in August 2011. No matter the degree to which it can later be construed as a possible training exercise — lessons to be learnt, etc. — it is astonishing to us that commentaries in the year since have not considered what a month, two months or more of "uprising" along the lines of Tunisia, Egypt or even Quebec might entail for London. Indeed, it surprises us that in academic commentary only textbook approaches have been countenanced. The LSE/Guardian research to "read" the riots (see Roberts 2011) involved a large number of interviews with people claiming to have engaged in rioting and looting. We have to leave aside the sedentary apolitical stance of merely *reading* riots here — indeed, we think *more* reading is required, not of the "social as text", but rather of some politi-

---

20. "Gangster who joined millionaire's daughter Laura Johnson on looting spree jailed for dealing crack cocaine" Telegraph April 5, 2012 — http://www.telegraph.co.uk/news/uknews/crime/9188299/Gangster-who-joined-millionaires-daughter-Laura-Johnson-on-looting-spree-jailed-for-dealing-crack-cocaine.html — retrieved August 27 2012.
21. Many thanks to our colleague, and prisons expert, Sophie Fuggle for comments that have helped further this text.

cal theory texts, for example, and in a critical way, the commentaries we have been examining here. We approach "Reading the Riots" with caution against its staging of verbatim reportage, its citation-quotation-ventriloquy, and its from-the-curb authenticity claims. Despite the scale and profile of the Guardian/LSE project, it appears, as Iossifidis and Thomas (2012) note, that the authors of the research fail to assert the veracity of their work from claims that you cannot trust the views expressed by the participants as they were criminals. We are particularly interested that one of the key findings of the "Reading the Riots" research was that much "behaviour" was motivated by hatred of the police. Yet, the analysis of the interviews with those involved in the uprising fails at the same time to broach any stated motives for police-hatred in the context of neoliberal labour market "control". If it is the case that *many* of the research participants described their first-hand experiences of police brutality, racialised and classed discrimination, indiscriminate stop and search, and the extra judiciary killing of Mark Duggan, it is then underwhelming that the researchers meekly assert that;

> One reason for hostility towards the police could be that two-thirds of those interviewed said they had been cautioned by the police or convicted of an offence in the past. The riots provided a long-sought opportunity for settling scores (Roberts 2011).

The Guardian/LSE study blames antagonism towards the police upon the participants' previous criminal histories and not on the police's role as defenders of class hierarchy, defenders of capital and keepers of an unjust peace. Yet, the police are looking at major cuts after years of corruption, bad press, scandals — de Menezes, deaths in custody — and failures of process, racism within the force, taking bribes and kickbacks, selling the drugs they confiscate, farming out actual work to subcontracted half-beats and leaning on the Police Federation to present them as human. In an exemplary initiative, the Association of Chief Police Officers attempted their own diversionary tactic to distract from the Police's perceived failings at putting down the insurrection;

> August also showed the ability of the police to restore order using robust, common sense policing in the British way (Prasad 2011).

The idea that there is a specifically British mode of policing — the redoubtful Bobby — is mockery in the extreme, flying in the face of the control function required from the Force today. Even if it remains astonishing that there can be any residual "moral" expectation that the police behave with respect and decency, widespread awareness and realisation that this cannot be the case in the era of austerity prevails. The fictional and amiable Bobby does not kill in custody, does not do the bidding of the Employers Federation, does not stand by while peoples' houses burn, does not mount water cannon, Jankel battle trucks, or threaten armed response in the mythos of a "British way" of policing. In this fantasy, protests would be respected, injustices repaired and cops who kill would go to court and prison. The moral expectation here is not just a media phenomenon, nor can it be reduced to ethnicity, community or democratic values — it flies in the face of the evidence of the Police as a violent force of control, and August 2011 was yet another one of its thousand nadirs.

This Police public relations crisis is where we see a distinct break from the previous occasion the Conservative party entered Downing Street. When Margaret Thatcher came to power in 1979, her Home Secretary (William Whitelaw, 1st Viscount Whitelaw, KT, CH, MC, PC, DL) famously hugely improved police pay and conditions. The police obviously felt indebted to the incoming Conservative Government for their new conservatories, which enabled the political deployment of the police throughout the 1981 uprisings, the miners' strike and the battle of Wapping.[22] Whitelaw was the Home Secretary whose term covered the summer when London, and England, was again burning, with large-scale disturbances in Liverpool, Birmingham, Manchester, Sheffield, Leeds and several areas of London. Whitelaw also implemented the expensive and ineffectual policy of the "short, sharp, shock" for young offenders. In contrast today, the Police are feeling "despised" by the UK Government's attack on their pensions, resources and working practices (Tully 2012).

As Sukant Chandan writes, the "youth have been without effective guidance".[23] If there was a Left resurgence, it might fight for the permanent dismantling of any possibility of such state renegade/retrogressive opportunist — training programme/pogrom — activity. The youth of August 2011 showed how capital can be threatened, irrespective of analysis and theory. It remains to be seen if the commentators and "programmes", role models and workfare, uniforms and prisons, can quash this spirit. Our complaint is that in place of theoretically and politically informed analysis, what we were offered instead was not so much inadequate, as plain misdirection. For example, the focus upon new media, as shown in "Reading the Riots" (Roberts 2011), and in nearly every media report at the time and since (e.g. BBC Radio Four August 7, 2011, BBC Newsnight August 12, 2011, Guardian July 4, 2012,[24] etc.), presented the uprising as an electronic contagion, effectively eschewing context altogether, though also linking the uprisings to some of the more fanciful stories about the

---

22. In another text, we might render the Newspaper Baron of Wapping as a Harkonnen leader from the Planet Dune, perhaps a Dark Lord. His fall from grace before the Leveson Inquiry, with his Number One Son having to take the sword — he only Johnny Marbles' well-aimed pie — brings the allegory neatly home.

23. See his text on the riots and black youth organisation at http://sonsofmalcolm.blogspot.co.uk/2012/08/black-power-perspective-on-2011-aug.html — retrieved August 29, 2012

24. Actually, the *Guardian* report on custodial sentences is an exemplar of horrific numeration. Cold graphs and pie-charts document the 3000 plus incarcerations, with an average custodial sentence of 16 months. This is a statistical bludgeoning that beggars belief. Admirable perhaps that readers are left to draw their own conclusions, but it is still the case that wider contextualisation is not broached — "Riots broken down: who was in court and what's happened to them" Guardian July 4, 2012 — http://www.guardian.co.uk/news/datablog/2012/jul/04/riot-defendants-court-sentencing — retrieved August 29, 2012

Arab Spring, but without really offering an analysis of this and the way those events were a culmination of many years of organisation. The new media explanation in particular appears almost as if it were an advertising campaign for Twitter, Blackberry and Facebook, but with no critique of these media companies as profit-making concerns. The rebranding of social media as political tool was stalled at the same time, in a hand-wringing anxiety that again sat mesmerised before a youth culture it could not understand, but wanted still to subsume.

Clerical-Hysterical

We have identified a series of mind tricks that distract us from what is substantially at stake in the wake of the uprisings of August 2011. The deceptions are to some degree intended, but also tinged with self-serving denial, complicity and cynical myopia. This is the art of politics, just as much as it is Jedi duplicity. One set of arguments we have made would suggest that the "rioters" are portrayed within a framework of stereotype and racism. Another set of arguments suggest that these riots were exactly the riots we had to have — the ground for the disturbances was prepared by a commodity celebrity culture where role models are vacuous and the equation of value to exchange is a threadbare fiction — new trainers and sports clothes from Primark do not make the cut. Other commentators would have us look elsewhere to say we have seen it all before, and we agree, but think that a mere gestural reference to austerity does not get to the heartless heart of the Big Society. In a year of commentary, the production of a class of complicit pundits, more or less in the pay of property, capital and privilege, amounts to a more or less "obvious campaign to white-wash the uprising, to turn it into anything but resistance to the deeply white supremacist nature of this country".[25] The story is more complicated, yet the truth more simple: Capital in a time of crisis needs a good cop bad cop routine, bread and circuses, and fire and brimstone. There were two Augusts: we have the Olympics and the gangs to dissuade us from really having a look at what ruling class tricks have us ensnared.

Our assessment is that a major unacknowledged force hides behind the machinations that have brought us the Big Society and its symbiotic twins, the August riots, the Olympic distraction. Alongside this, a military juridical persecution and surveillance state that has armed the capital, drills its youth into the discipline of low-paid labour or internships in sweated service sectors, uniforms or jail. There is an escalated persecution complex that has just cause in that black and Asian youth are stopped in the street, demonised in the press and pilloried in the dock by a white supremacist and racist co-ordination that brooks no opposition. And there is next to no wider public opposition to this

---

25. Chandan, http://sonsofmalcolm.blogspot.co.uk/2012/08/black-power-perspective-on-2011-aug.html — retrieved August 29 2012.

because the pundits and commentators will not face the ways rhetorical flourish breeds complicity and protects property. The economic imperative couples with the control society. No-one can deny that many young people hate the police with good cause. A death in custody was the trigger, but stop and search, surly attitudes, bus dragnets, corruption, payola and more, while not endearing to police to anyone, were not the only operative factors. A wider agenda underpins the particularities of the day. Racism and class war act as a diversionary, hardly recognised, all-too-impactful deceit and distraction. We saw it on our screens, but could not name it as the Fire Brigades and Police were defending prime property while letting lesser capital burn. What an outrage, but only to be expected given where we are just now in the volatile process of cyclical accumulation. The valorisation/conversion of expropriated surplus value through circulation within a stag-flationary recession that favours write-offs and fire-sales means petit bourgeois traders suffer alongside the lumpenised masses. Meanwhile, big Capital strives to recoup what minimal profit can be scarpered away before the fire-sale season ends. The super rich survive, so far only slightly singed by the scandals, to then pounce to buy up the scorched earth as a bloody trophy upon which a new phase of accumulation is inaugurated. Class and location maps onto race and privilege to differentiate the cartography of valorised capital under the restructuring, the so-call "crisis" we are all in together. An alternative is brewing, and we write this looking for another hot August.

References

Cameron, D. (2011a) Cameron declares war on gangs. Retrieved from http://www.telegraph.co.uk/news/politics/david-cameron/8701853/England-riots-David-Cameron-declares-war-on-gangs.html.

Cameron, D. (2011b) *David Cameron on Bullingdon Club. Today Programme*, BBC, London.

Cameron, D. (2011c) Statement on the UK riots. Retrieved from http://www.guardian.co.uk/uk/2011/aug/09/david-cameron-full-statement-uk-riots.

Casey, L. (2012) *Listening to Troubled Families*, HM Department for Communities and Local Government, London.

Centre for Social Justice (2012) *Time to Wake Up: Tackling Gang One Year after the Riots*, Centre for Social Justice, London.

Chatterjee, P. (1997) *A Possible India: Essays in Political Criticism*, Oxford University Press, Oxford.

Cohen, S. & Young, J. (eds) (1981) *The Manufacture of News: Social Problems, Deviancy and the Mass Media*, Constable, London.

Hutnyk, J (2011) 'Pantomine Paranoia in London, or, 'Look Out, He's Behind You'' in Peddie, I. (ed.), *Popular Music and Human Rights*, Ashgate, Farnham, pp. 51–65.

Iossifidis, M. & Thomas, P. (2012) *Reading the Riots: One Year On*. http://www.opendemocracy.net/ourkingdom/miranda-iossifidis-philippa-thomas/reading-riots-one-year-on retreieved 1st September 2012.

Jones, O. (2011) *Chavs: The Demonization of the Working Class*, Verso, London.

Khalid Qureshi Foundation and Chelsea Ives Youth Centre (2011) 'Riote Pol-Econ', *Mute Magazine*, vol. 3, no. 2, pp. 98-111.

King, J. (1996) *The Football Factory*, Jonathan Cape, London.

King, J. (1999) *England Away*, Jonathan Cape, London.

Laville, S. (2012) '16 Sentenced Over Night of Terror in West London', *The Guardian*, 9 Aug, http://www.guardian.co.uk/uk/2012/aug/08/rioters-notting-hill-ledbury-jailed (accessed 30 December 2012).

Maguire, J. (2004) *Understanding Psychology and Crime*, Open University Press, Maidenhead.

Marx, Karl (1867/1976) Capital. Volume One.

Mccarthy, D. (2011) 'Classing Early Intervention: Social Class, Occupational Moralities and Criminalization', *Critical Social Policy*, vol. 31, no. 4, pp. 495-516.

McCoy, A. (2009) *Policing America's Empire: The United States, The Philippines and The Rise of the Surveillance State*, University of Wisconsin Press, Madison, WI.

Mitropoulos, Angela (2007) 'Notes on the Frontiers and Borders of the Postcolony', in Narula, M., Shuddhabrata, S., Jeebesh, B. & Ravi, S. (eds) *Frontiers – Sarai Reader 07*, Sarai, New Delhi, pp. 372-380.

Mitropoulos, Angela (2012) 'Proliferating Limits: The Oikonomic Limits of Capitalist Dynamics and Technologies of the Border', in Hutnyk, John (ed.) *Beyond Borders*, Pavement Books, London.

Phillips, T. (2005) *After 7/7: Sleepwalking to Segregation*, Commission for Racial Equality, London.

Pickard, J. (2010) Exclusive: David Cameron and the Bullingdon Night of the Broken Window. Retrieved from http://blogs.ft.com/westminster/2010/04/exclusive-david-cameron-and-the-bullingdon-night-of-the-broken-window/.

Piper, C. (2011). The English Riots and Tough Sentencing. Retrieved from http://blog.oup.com/2011/09/tough-sentencing/.

Prasad, R. (2011) 'The Riots were 'A Sort Or Revenge' Against the Police', in Roberts, D. (ed.) *Reading the Riots*, The Guardian, London.

Prins, G. & Salisbury, R. (2008) 'Risk, Threat and Security: The Case of the UK', *RUSI*, vol. 153, no. 1, pp. 6-11.

Roberts, D. (ed.) (2011) *Reading the Riots*, The Guardian, London.

Sherman, J. (2012). 'Government Sends in the Scouts to Riot Hotspots'. *London: The Time*, 25 Aug., p. 1.

Singh, D. (2012) *After the Riots: The final Report of the Riots, Communities and Victims Panel*, Riots, communities and victims panel, London.

Singleton, A. (2011) Update: Riots and Area Deprivation. Retrieved 24 April, 2012, from http://www.alex-singleton.com/?p=519.

Star Wars episode IV: A New Hope (1977) dir. G. Lucas, motion picture, Hollywood.

Sykes, G. & Matza, D. (1993) *Techniques of Neutralization: A Theory of Delinquency*, Ardent Media, New York, NY.

Tully, J (2012) A Message from the Chairman. Retrieved 15 November, 2012, from http://www.metfed.org.uk/news?id=1904.

Van Bueren, G. & Woolley, S. (2010) *Stop and Think*, Equality and Human Rights Commission, London.

Vidal, G. (2002) *Perpetual War for Perpetual Peace. How We Got to be So Hated – Causes of Conflict in the Last Empire*, Claireview, Forest Row.

Willetts, D. (2011). England is Sick – Pole Monika Tells of Riot Blaze Hell. *London: The Sun*, 13 Aug., p. 1.

Index

Abaza, Mona 50
Abbot, Diane 47
Adorno, T. 13, 20, 47
affray 1-2
aftermath of riots 21-4
Al Aswany, Alaa 49-50, 53
Al Jazeera 53-4, 62
Al Khamissi, Khaled 49
Al-Fayed, Dodi 16
al-Thawra al-daHika 58
Alaidy, Ahmed 49
Albrow, Martin 46-8
Ali, Shazad 94, 98
alien mentality 73
American Geographical Society 9
Amin, Ash 1-2
amorality 56, 68, 105
anarchy 67
"anti-black riots" 31
anti-dictatorship 63
anti-intellectualism 3
anti-social behaviour orders 105
antipathy 32
apoplexy 20
Arab Spring 3, 20, 47, 57, 59, 115
arch-traditionalism 13
Armbrust, Walter 53-4, 62
ASBOs *see* anti-social behaviour orders
Asian youth 1-4, 27, 71, 90, 106
August 2011 riots 1-6, 29-32; events of 29-32; rapid reaction 4-6; in the shadow of riots 1; situating riots 1-4
austerity 27-8, 30, 35, 41-2, 76, 87-9, 100-101

Bakhtin, Mikhail 18
Ballard, J. D. 11
banality of street violence 88
barbarism 95
Barker, P. 8
Bateman, Tim 32
Batmanghelidj, Camila 56

Battle of Wapping 114
Bauman, Zygmunt 5, 13, 77-81
BBC 4-5, 9, 13-15, 18-19, 33-4, 105-6
Behr, Rafael 73
Benjamin, W. 47
Betjeman, John 8
Bhabha, Homi 32, 58
Big Society 5, 46-65, 100-110, 115-16; gated community 48-54; *see also* Cameron, David
Billig, M. 85-6
Bin Laden, Osama 97
Birbalsingh, K. 72
Birmingham 92-3
Blackhurst, R. 12, 23
Blair, Tony 23, 85
Blears, Hazel 19, 30
"bling-bling economy" 59-60
Blitz 12, 17
BNP *see* British National Party
Bouazizi, Mohamed 47-8
Bourdieu, Pierre 54
bourgeois utopia 14-15
Bradley, John 49-50, 53, 55, 59
brainwashing 11
Brando, Marlon 104
Briggs, D. 4
British National Party 16, 90
Britishness 8-9, 11-12, 85-99, 113-14
Brixton 27-33, 36, 39-41
broken Britain 30, 33, 48, 66-72, 85-7, 90-96, 104-6; and interracial violence 93; *see also* Cameron, David
Brown, Gordon 85
BS *see* Big Society
Bulger, Jamie 16
Bullingdon Club 105-6
Burchill, Julie 97
Burrell, Kingsley 89

Cairo Cosmopolitan 54
Cairo to Tottenham 46-65

INDEX

Callinicos, Alex 37
Cameron, David 5, 17-23, 27, 30, 35, 46, 57, 66-7, 85-7, 90-96, 104-111
Campaign for the Protection of Rural England 9
Cantle Report 74
capitalism 35-6
Casey, Louise 105, 108
causes of 1981 riots 32-4
Chandan, Sukant 114
Chang, Ha-Joon 48
Chelsea Ives Youth Centre 106
citizen journalism 18, 21
civil society 61-3
Clapham 2011 1-6
Clegg, Nick 109-110
clerical hysteria 115-16
Cliff, Tony 38-9
Cohen, S. 5, 18, 23
Collateral Damage 77-9
collective anger 37-8, 60
colonial utopias 46-65
community cohesion 74
concept of gang 104-8
consumer citizens 77-81
consumer culture 11-14
consumer-generated frustrations 81
consumerism 66-84; *see also* shopping with violence
consumption vs. consumerism 77-81
containment of threat 70-71
contested causes of 1981 riots 32-4
context flattening 68-71
contexts for distraction 100-117; clerical-hysterical 115-16; courting trouble 110-115; political gangs 104-6; race, control 106-8; shopping with violence 108-110
Cook, Robin 15
Counterfire 39-40
Counterpunch 57
courting trouble 110-115
Criminal Justice Bill 18
criminality 22, 26, 29-30, 36-8, 48, 52, 57, 66-75, 88-9
critical consumerism 66-84; conclusion 81; consumer citizens 77-81; flattening context 68-71; introduction 66-8; neoliberal response to policy 74-7; resilience of race 71-4
Croydon 7-11, 14-17, 19, 22-3, 29, 109-110
cyberspace 21
Czernik, A. 36

Daily Mail 4, 67, 92, 111
Daily Mirror 72
Daily Telegraph 72
Davis, Evan 105-6

Davis, Mike 54
Dean, James 104
decline of suburbia 17-21
deferred gratification 75
demise of capitalism 14
democratic accountability 75
demonisation 48, 56, 107
Denis, Eric 62-3
deregulation 48, 55-6
deterrence hypothesis 112
deviance 104-6, 110-115
diasporic suburbanisation 15
dictatorship 49, 54, 63
dignity 57-63
disavowal of suburbia 22
disconnection 19
disordered times 88-9
distraction 100-117
diverging entry points in narrative 39-41
dividing factors 4
Donaldson, S. 11
Duggan, Mark 1, 11-12, 20, 29-30, 47, 59, 66, 89-93, 102, 113
dumbing down 20-21
Duncan Smith, Ian 33-4
dysfunctional capitalism 4, 73, 100-102, 109
dystopian vision 7-8, 61

Ealing 9-19, 21-3, 108
Ealing Gazette 12
Economist 80
EDL *see* English Defence League
Efford, Clive 17
Egypt 46-65
Eighteenth Brumaire of Louis Bonaparte 26-7
El Shenawy, Karim 53
electronic contagion 114
elitism 30, 50
Ellis, Clough William 9
Encoding-Decoding Theory 21
end of English dream 7-25
English Defence League 17
entry points in narrative 39-41
escapism 14-17
ethnic vote 15
ethnicity 4
euphoria 60
Evening Standard 12
event of "riots" 87-8
events of August 2011 29-32
everyday nationhood 98
expenses scandal 12, 19, 57
experience economy 79

Facebook 4-6, 13, 16, 19, 115
Fanon, F. 49

INDEX

Farah, Mo 4
Farrar, M. 90
"fat cats" 49-52, 57-8
"feel-bad" viewing 5
feral youth 12, 70, 91
fiction of whiteness 90
15M Movement 103
flash points 47-8, 56-7, 102-3
flashmob 19
flattening of context 68-71
Florida, Richard 80
folk devils 5, 18-19, 23
Folk Devils and Moral Panics 18
football violence 104-6, 888
forgotten families 76, 93-4
framing the suburb 7-11
Frankfurt School 20
Fraser, Demetre 89
freeloading generation 12
French counter-revolution 27
French Revolution 27
Frost, D. 31, 33
frustrations 81

G20 68
Gallagher, Liam 20, 69
Galloway, George 36
Gandhi, Indira 104
gang activity 66-8, 104-8, 115-16
gated community 48-54
gender self-assertion 59-60
German, L. 39
Giddens, Anthony 20-21
Gilroy, Paul 27, 72-3
Goldberg, D. 93
Goldworthy, V. 22
good and bad Muslims 97-8
good Brummie, bad Brummmie 94-7
"good rioting" 3
Goodhart, D. 72-3
Gordon Riots 1780 39-40
Gove, Michael 61
Grainger, Anthony 89
grand narrative 39-41
"Green Unrest" 39
Grossmith, G. 8
Grossmith, W. 8
Guardian, the 5, 10-11, 15, 27-8, 41-2, 54-5, 75, 109, 112-14

Hall, Stuart 21, 54-5, 58
Halloran, J. 21
Hallsworth, S. 34, 41
Hammoudan, Mohamed 58
Hanieh, Adam 53
Harman, Chris 37-8
Harvey, David 52, 70
Hatherley, O. 80

hedonism 68, 72
Hegel, Georg Wilhelm Friedrich 26-7
Henshner, P. 34
hip-hop 73
Hirschler, S. 31
history vs. farce 26-45
Hobsbawm, Eric 13
Holgate, Jane 62
hooliganism 31
Hoover, J. Edgar 104
Hughes, S. 28, 33-4
Hunt, T. 8
hysteria 115-16

identifying beginning and end 89-90
IMF *see* International Monetary Fund
"imported Jamaican culture" 72-3
in the shadow of riots 1
Independent, The 34
indie music 7-8
indignados 89
information overload 13
injustice 30, 90-92, 98
Inside Egypt 49-50
institutional racism 41-2, 93
International Monetary Fund 53, 62
International Socialism 37-8
interracial violence 40, 93, 98
intervention programmes 108
Iossifidis, M. 133
Ishkanian, Armine 48
Islam 16, 93-4
issue of shopping with violence 108-110

Jahan, Haroon 94-8
Jahan, Tariq 5, 71, 97-8
Jedi *see Star Wars*
Jefferson, T. 31
Jenkins, Roy 95
Jhally, S. 14
Johnson, Boris 1, 3, 13, 17, 20, 22, 105
Johnson, Laura 16
Johnson, Lyndon B. 104
Jones, J. 40
Jones, Owen 105

Kamel, Nagui 58
karama 59; *see also* dignity
Kennedy, John 104
Khalid Qureshi Foundation 106
killing of Mark Duggan 1, 11-12, 20, 29-30, 47, 59, 66, 89-93, 102, 113
King Lear 5, 66-7, 81
King, Sadie 56
Kingston 7-11
Kingston Guardian 10
Konczyk, Monika 110
Kunzru, Hari 19, 79-80

INDEX

Labidi, Lilia 58-9
Lammy, David 4, 17
Lawrence, Stephen 94
Lea, J. 34, 41
Lehman Brothers 109
Lentin, A. 15, 76
lessons from riots 34-9
Lewis, P. 27
lived multiculturalism 93
living in time of disorder 88-9
London Riots 100-101; *see also* August 2011 riots
London Road 9, 11, 17
Londonstani 59
looting 11, 15-16, 33, 57-60, 66-9, 110-111
lost society 61-3
Lowenthal, D. 9

Mccarthy, D. 105
McDonald, K. 32-3
McDonnell, John 57
McRobbie, A. 23
Mafhouz, Asmaa 48
Maguire, J. 112
Major, John 20
Malkani, Gautam 59
Mamdani, M. 95
Manchester 2011 66-84
marginalisation 90
Marks & Spencer 11
Marx, Karl 26-7, 102
May, Theresa 27, 57
Mbembe, A. 79-80
"me-tooism" mimicry 59
mediation 78
Mehrez, Samia 60-61
Mercury, Freddy 86
Merry, John 75
Metcalf, J. 27
Metro 12
Miliband, Ed 20
Militant 40
mind tricks 4, 100-101, 106-8, 115-16
Mitchell, Timothy 50, 52-3, 62
modern moral panic 17-21
modern protest 77-81
Monk, Daniel Bertrand 54
moral bankruptcy 17-18
moral panic 5, 7-25, 30-31
morality substitute 78
Morning Star 2-3, 33-4, 36
Morrissey 7-8
Mubarak, Hosni 46-65
muggings 19
mukhabarat 48-54
multiculturalism 3-4, 17, 22-4, 90, 94-5, 106
Murji, K. 68

Musavir, Abdul 94, 98
Muslim Brotherhood 52-3
Muslim families 93-4, 97-8; good and bad Muslims 97-8
"Muslim rage" 63

narcissism 59
National Front 40-41
nationalism 85-6, 90-92, 107
NATO 103
Neal, S. 68
neo-Darwinian survival 101-2
neo-moral panic 5, 7-25
neoliberal response to policy 74-7
neoliberal states 46-65; flash points 47-8; gated communities 48-54; lost vs. civil society 61-3; revolutionary language 57-61; shrunken society 54-7
neoliberal utopianism 54
neoliberalism 13, 53-8
nepotism 49
Nestlé 11
New Labour 15, 20, 23
New Left Review 23
New Statesman 73
Newburn, T. 27, 67
Newsnight 11, 15, 72
Newsweek 63
nihilism 68, 72-3
Nixon, Richard 104
Notting Hill 31, 40

Obama, Barack 15, 97-8
Oborne, Peter 12-13
Occupy 62, 86
O'Dwyer, Michael 40
Olympic Games 3-5, 17, 21, 23-4, 79, 85-6, 94, 98, 107, 110, 112, 115
O'Neill, B. 33
Ovenden, K. 36

Page, John 62
paleoconservatism 73; *see also* Starkey, David
palimpsestic narrative 38
palliative care 101
Panorama 33
paraphrasing Hegel 26-7
Parsons, T. 72
PCC *see* Police Complaints Commission
Pearson, G. 30-31
Peasants' Revolt 1381 39-40
Phillips, R. 31, 33
Pickles, Eric 14
Pilgrim, Liz 12
Police Complaints Commission 34, 102
policy 74-7
"policy-as-jargon" 55

INDEX

political gangs 104-6
political subjectivity 77-81
poll tax riots 31, 40
Polyani, K. 54
popular culture 47
possessive individualism 58
post-race riots 14-17
post-racial fantasies 85-99; event of "riots" 87-8; good Brummie, bad Brummie 94-7; good Muslim, bad Muslim 97-8; identifying beginning and end 89-90; interracial violence 93; living in disordered times 88-9; Muslim families 93-4; regionalisation of unrest 90-92; space of race 92-3; street violence 88; 2012 98
Powell, Enoch 17, 92
Power, N. 41
pride 57-61
Prince, J. 9
public disorder 31, 41-2, 80-81, 85-92, 94-5
Public Order Act 1994 18, 106

Queen's Jubilee 85-6, 112

Race & Class 34, 40-41
race and control 106-8
"race riots" 1-4, 14-17, 31-2, 62-3, 90-92
racial mixing 17
racial resilience 71-4
"racist tram video" 9
rapid reaction 4-6
Reading the Riots 27, 29-30, 41, 109, 112-14
Reagan, Ronald 104
rebellious crowd 32
Rees, J. 39
regional narratives 85-99
regionalisation of unrest 90-92
relevance of riots 7-11
remaining a good Muslim 98
repeating Thatcherism 34-9
resilience of race 71-5
resistance 34-9
"revolution of the joke" 58
revolutionary language 57-61
Richardson, B. 33, 35
riot as event 87-8
riotous language 57-61
Riots 56, 60-61
riots as resistance 34-9
riots in retrospect 21-4
Roberts, Kenneth 39
Roosevelt, Franklin D. 104
Rowell, Andy 22
Royal Family 8
Rudé, George 32

running riot in Manchester 66-84

Said, Khaled 47-8
Salafi 53
Sayer, A. 78-9
Scarman Report 67, 74
segregation 106
self-affirmation 78-80
self-congratulation 85
self-esteem 50, 60
self-help 58
self-identity 78
self-respect 60
self-satisfaction 10
self-sufficiency 52, 54, 75
sheer criminality 57, 67
shopping with violence 5, 11, 66-84, 100-101, 108-110; "shopping riots" 66-84
shrunken society 54-7
shunning 48
Singh, Udham 40
Singleton, A. 111
Sissay, Lemn 57, 59
situating riots 1-4
Sivanandan, A. 34, 40
slavery 22
sleepwalking to segregation 106
Slovo, Gillian 56, 59-61
"slurred treatises" 106-8
Smiley Culture 89
Smith, E. 29, 32
Smith, Jacqui 19
Social Action and Research Foundation 75
social crisis 71, 104-6
Socialism Today 35
Socialist Review 35
Socialist Worker 34
Socialist Workers Party 35-40
Solomos, J. 72
space of race 92-3
spectre of summer '81 26-45; causes of 1981 riots 32-4; conclusion 41-2; diverging entry points 39-41; events of August 2011 29-32; Thatcherism repeats itself 34-9
Spivak, G. 38
Stacey, Jason 14
Star Wars 4, 100-101, 104-6, 115; *see also* mind tricks
Starkey, David 4, 11, 15, 17, 72-3
Stevenson, B. 36
stigmatisation 36-7
stop and search policy 27-8, 56, 76
street violence 88
structuration 20-21
subjectivity 77-81
suburban aftermath 21-4

INDEX

suburbia running riot 7-25; consumer culture 11-14; modern moral panic 17-21; post-race riots 14-17; relevance of riots 7-11; suburban aftermath 21-4
summer 1981 26-45
Surrey Comet 10
surveillance 55-6, 76, 102-3, 112, 115-16
SWP *see* Socialist Workers Party
Szreter, Simon 48

Terrorism Act 2000 106
Thatcher, Margaret 22, 26-7, 38-9, 114
Thatcherism 22, 34-9, 41-2
Thermidor period 27
Thomas, Gareth 23
Thomas, P. 113
Time Out 12
Titley, G. 76
Tottenham 12, 18-19, 21, 29-32, 39, 46-65, 108
Towfik, Ahmed 49-54, 61
Toynbee, P. 20
trade union movement 37-8
tragedies of Muslim families 93-4
"Trumpton Riots" 8
turning a blind eye 47-8
Twitter 4-6, 10-11, 13, 16-19, 23, 115
tyranny 55

Un-American Activities Commission 104
underclasses 34-6, 41-2, 48, 56, 72-3, 100-101
United Kingdom *see* August 2011 riots

urban dysfunction 7-8
utopia 46-65
Utopia 49-52, 54-5, 61

van Zoonen, L. 21
vandalism 30, 33, 73-4
vengeance 97-8
vigilantism 71
violent policing 100-102
Voice, The 17

Waddington, P. 31
Walker, D. 20
"War on Poverty" 104
war on terror 102-3, 107
Waters, M. 21
Watson, Stephen 19
Weekly Worker 36
West, Johnny 59
Wheatle, A. 27-8, 34
White City Television Centre 9-10
white supremacy 4
Whitelaw, Willie 27, 114
Wicks, Malcolm 7, 11
Winson Green *see* Birmingham
Wootton, Charles 40
Wretched of the Earth 49

Yacoubian Building 49
Young, T. 72
YouTube 3, 13, 54

Žižek, Slavoj 5, 13, 53, 68